A Historian's Guide to Copyright

by Michael Les Benedict

ABOUT THE AUTHOR: Michael Les Benedict is an emeritus professor of history at Ohio State University, the parliamentarian for the American Historical Association, and a member of the AHA's Task Force on Intellectual Property. Benedict received his B.A. and M.A. degrees from the University of Illinois and his Ph.D. from Rice University. He has contributed several crucial works to the field of Civil War and Reconstruction studies, including *The Impeachment and Trial of Andrew Johnson* (1973), *A Compromise of Principle: Congressional Republicans and Reconstruction, 1863–1869* (1975), *Fruits of Victory: Alternatives in Restoring the Union, 1865–1877* (1986), and *Preserving the Constitution: Essays on Politics and the Constitution in the Reconstruction Era* (2006). He is also the author of *The Blessings of Liberty* and other works on American constitutional history.

AHA EDITORS: Robert B. Townsend and Sarah Fenton

LAYOUT AND COVER DESIGN: Christian A. Hale

© 2012 by the American Historical Association
ISBN: 978-0-87229-180-5

Published in 2012 by the American Historical Association. As publisher, the American Historical Association does not adopt official views on any field of history and does not necessarily agree or disagree with the views expressed in this book.

Library of Congress Cataloging-in-Publication Data:

Benedict, Michael Les.

A historian's guide to copyright / Michael Les Benedict.

p. cm.

Includes bibliographical references.

ISBN 978-0-87229-180-5

1. Copyright--United States. 2. Historians--United States--Handbooks, manuals, etc. I. Title.

KF2995.B46 2012   346.7304'82--dc23

2012005723

TABLE OF CONTENTS

ACKNOWLEDGEMENTS

Several colleagues have gone out of their way to help complete this brief work. Sanford Thatcher, the former director of the Pennsylvania State University Press, past president of the American Association of University Publishers, and longtime chair of its Committee on Copyright, drew upon his great fund of knowledge to comment on the penultimate draft. Craig Joyce, Andrews Kurth Professor of Law at the University of Houston Law School and co-director of its Institute for Intellectual Property & Information Law, did likewise. They not only advised on the law but suggested editorial changes that clarified and tightened the prose. The project has benefited from the patient oversight of Stanley N. Katz, the chairperson of the American Historical Association's Task Force on Intellectual Property (TFIP), who has made so many contributions to American scholarly life during his career on the faculties of the University of Chicago School of Law and the Woodrow Wilson School at Princeton University, and as the president of the American Council of Learned Societies. I am also grateful for the encouragement offered by TFIP members Michael Grossberg and Page Putnam Miller, and by Robert B. Townsend, the AHA's deputy director, and the AHA's executive director James Grossman. While the work that follows owes so much to the advice of these generous colleagues, the shortcomings are my own.

THE PURPOSE OF THIS GUIDE

This pamphlet is intended as a basic primer on copyright for historians. It deals with copyright as it relates to research, publication, and teaching. It looks back over the history of copyright law, establishes a foothold on a field now very much in flux, and looks ahead to a changed landscape. It does not provide advice about particular situations, even common ones, for which historians should consult a literary agent and/or a lawyer. Academic historians might also check to see whether theirs is one of many universities that have put copyright guides available online for their faculty and students. But they are not aimed at specialists in particular disciplines.

Copyright law establishes the rights of authors and other creators, and those who have acquired their rights, to control the public distribution of their work for a fixed duration, and subject to limitations. Once a legal backwater, copyright is currently one of the most dynamic and knotty areas of law—part of the field now called "intellectual property," which also includes the law of patents, trademarks, trade secrets, and areas of the law dealing with human knowledge, personality, and ideas. Driving this change are the explosive increase in the value of information in an "Information Age"; the rise of new technologies for the distribution of that information; the dynamic growth of the entertainment industries; and the centrality to the digital revolution of computer programs, which are creative, written expressions, and thus subject to copyright. These developments have coincided with a revived sympathy for property rights in American law and politics, efforts to protect intellectual property in a globalized economy, and a movement to harmonize American copyright law with international copyright law, which traditionally has secured greater rights to creators. The control of copyright owners has expanded at the expense of users. Historians are both.

A guide to copyright must therefore account for rival conceptions of its character and purpose. One school sees copyright as a limited set of rights designed primarily to encourage the creative process and the dissemination of its products. This school stresses the need to circulate those products widely, easily, and to some degree freely. A second school of thought proceeds from the view that people are morally entitled to the fruits of their labor and sees copyright primarily as a tool to secure those rights—thereby interpreting owners' copyrights broadly and users' rights narrowly. Even more trenchantly, publishers, distributors, and their lawyers see creative productions as "intellectual property," whose "owners" are entitled to maximize its value, to demand payment for its use, and to control its distribution, just like the owners of any other property. Easy circulation takes second place in this view to the rights held by creators and distributors to reap the economic value of their property.[1]

Historians and their publishers can be found on both sides of this issue. As creators, they are keen to control and profit from their creations. As users they need easy access to historical information and interpretation and the freedom to use both in teaching, research, and their own publications.

The American copyright regime has been important to historians as writers, protecting our publications and preventing others from simply usurping their distribution. This is what gives our manuscripts value when we negotiate agreements with publishers. Copyright also governs our use of published and unpublished materials in our research and writing. But until recently, most historians have not found it necessary to learn very much about this aspect of the subject. We quoted primary and secondary sources in our books and articles without much worrying about copyright issues, and our publishers raised no objections as long as we assumed responsibility for getting permissions where necessary—and it rarely seemed necessary. We photocopied with abandon. With the creation of the Internet, we freely cut excerpts from original postings and pasted them into our own notes, we downloaded whole articles and stored them on our hard drives, and we put source materials online for all to use.

Most historians paid just as little attention to copyright in teaching, generally assuming the right to distribute copyrighted work to our classes, as long as the purpose was educational and not for our profit. We put photocopied excerpts from books on reserve for our students. We showed slides and movies in class, and we played records. We photocopied primary and secondary sources, put them in course packets, and told students to buy them at local copy shops. As technology has grown more sophisticated, we have put classroom materials on "electronic reserve" maintained by our libraries, or have put them on our websites or on websites dedicated to particular classes.

But things are changing and are going to change more. In the new Information Age, in which lawyers refer to creative works, ideas, and expressions as "intellectual property," information has value. Those who have the right to control its distribution can realize that value by restricting access in two ways. First, they have developed gatekeeping technologies, especially to electronically transmitted information and creations. Second, they have used the law to enforce copyrights—expanding the scope of what is covered, extending the term for which rights are protected, and increasing penalties for violations. Both alternatives limit historians' ability to use sources as freely as they have in the past, and the second can lead to litigation and damages. Even if an infringement does little real damage to a copyright owner, Congress has established statutory damages that can mount significantly.

Many provisions of copyright law protect researchers and educators from its full force. One can make "fair use" of copyrighted material in limited amounts and for proper purposes. Educators can make use of materials in the classroom in ways that others cannot. Libraries are secured a variety of privileges that serve historians and other patrons. Educators are spared some serious damages and costs if they reasonably believed themselves to be acting within the law. But ignorance of the law does not excuse an infringement; "reasonable belief" requires knowledge. The historian who does not know what the law requires and what it permits cannot claim that he thought his use was legally justified. Worse, by our actions, historians may induce students to infringe copyrights, putting them at risk as well.

The danger of litigation was remote in the past. It is still fairly remote today. But it is getting more immediate, and the possibility will continue to grow as stricter enforcement of copyrights becomes the norm. Because our institutions want to avoid litigation and liability, they may begin to impose restrictions on what we can do as teachers and scholars that go beyond what is necessary to comply with the law. In compensation, historians—or our publishers—will have stronger control over our copyrighted work. A basic knowledge of copyright is now essential.

THE EVOLUTION OF COPYRIGHT

Copyright emerged from the monopoly over the publication of printed works that Queen Mary granted in 1557 to the Company of Stationers—an English guild of text writers, illuminators, booksellers, and printers. The company's rules gave the original printer of any work a perpetual monopoly over its future publication—a "copyright" that could be bought and sold. In exchange for their monopoly, the stationers helped authorities censor publications by cooperating with a system of prior licensing. The system acquired statutory footing with the passage of the Licensing Act of 1662, one of the reactionary measures that accompanied the restoration of the Stuart monarchy after the Puritan Revolution and Cromwellian interregnum. But renegade printers challenged the system in the later 1600s; Parliament repealed the Licensing Act in 1681; and the stationers failed to get their charter renewed when it expired in 1695. The elimination of the old system led to wholesale pirating and the collapse of prior censorship. The still-powerful stationers urged Parliament to restore the old system, but anticensorship and antimonopoly feeling won out, and in 1710 Parliament passed a statute referred to in copyright history as the Statute of Anne, vesting copyright in authors instead of publishers. Rather than re-establish a perpetual monopoly, Parliament restricted the duration of copyright to a limited term after publication—only fourteen years.

Thus statutory copyright began as a reaction against efforts to maintain monopoly control over publication. That heritage seems to militate against the ever-increasing protection of intellectual property rights that has characterized recent decades. But the history of copyright in the United States took a different course. For most of the colonial period nearly all books and pamphlets had to be imported. But the number of colonial printers began to grow in the middle of the eighteenth century. They were not subject to the Statute of Anne, which did not apply to the American colonies. Although Massachusetts passed a law forbidding the reprinting of works without their owner's permission in 1672 (more than thirty years before Parliament's copyright statute), in general American printers simply published what they wanted. In the nation's founding years, Noah Webster, America's first great print entrepreneur, had to work diligently to persuade the new states to extend copyright protection to his highly popular, much pirated grammar and spelling books. His campaign persuaded the Constitution's framers to authorize Congress to establish copyrights and patents "for limited Times" in order "to promote the Progress of Science and useful Arts"—antimonopoly language inherited by the revolutionary generation from their radical Whig forbears. This language suggested that copyright was intended not to protect the property rights of inventors and creators, but rather to encourage technological and scientific development by rewarding creators for their efforts. On the other hand, Congress certainly was responding to the desire of authors like Webster to protect their property rights against pirates.

Congress began to fulfill this mandate immediately, passing the first copyright statute in 1790.[2] But while U.S. law protected American authors, it did not protect foreigners. American publishers regularly pirated foreign work, and foreign nations refused to protect American works from similar treatment within their boundaries. It took years of lobbying by luminaries such as Samuel L. Clemens (Mark Twain) and James Russell Lowell to persuade Congress to extend copyright protection to the works of foreigners. There was no prospect that the United States would join other nations in signing the international copyright agreement—the Berne Convention of 1886. Further lobbying led to new codifications that broadened the categories of creative works protected to include new technologies such as photography, phonographic recording, and moving pictures. These revisions culminated in the most recent and comprehensive law, the Copyright Act of 1976, which went into effect in 1978.[3] Augmented by amendments, especially the Digital Millennium Copyright Act of 1998,[4] the 1976 act remains the basis for copyright today. The U.S. finally became a party to the property rights-oriented Berne Convention in 1989 and has modified its laws to conform to its provisions.[5]

Thus American copyright reflects not only the antimonopoly heritage of Great Britain, but also the demands that Congress protect authors' rights to profit from their own creations, exposing a built-in tension between the desire to make creative work broadly available to society on the one hand, and the hunger for maximum freedom to exploit the financial potential of creative work on the other. Both Congress and the courts have worked to adjust this tension—Congress by provisions of the copyright statutes, and the courts by their interpretation.

Court interpretation of the statutes is particularly important, and has reflected the spirit of the times. Although nearly all copyright law is now based on federal statute,[6] the wording of some provisions—especially the all-important provision authorizing fair use of copyright materials—is purposely vague, giving courts broad leeway in applying it to particular cases. In the liberal environment of the 1960s and 1970s, the courts took a broad view of the public's interest in access to copyrighted work. With the more recent, conservative emphasis on property rights, uses that once might have been considered fair (or to have fallen within other exemptions) have been considered infringements instead.

GENERAL PRINCIPLES AND RULES OF COPYRIGHT

WHAT IS COPYRIGHT?

Copyright is the right of authors, artists, composers, and other creators, or those they designate, to control the reproduction, adaptation, distribution, display, and performance of the works they create. Copyright is a statutory right and is defined and enforced entirely through the copyright laws of the United States.[7] Even the provisions of the Berne Convention, to which the United States is now a party, must be enforced through changes made in the federal law to conform to it. However, American enforcement stops at the border. An author whose work is published in another country, or whose work is infringed there, must enforce his rights in that country, which probably is also a signatory of the Berne Convention.

Copyright only protects what is covered by the law and in the way the law specifies. The law permits people to use copyrighted works without permission in a variety of circumstances and under limitations set by the law itself. Publishers, authors, or broadcasters may seek to impose stricter limitations than the law does, or to impose their own interpretations of the law. They may declare that a book, unpublished paper, or televised event is subject to copyright and cannot be quoted or reproduced in any way without express consent. Publishers and educators may negotiate and publish guidelines about how copyrighted works may be used. Copyright owners' representatives may post authoritative-sounding statements that teachers must secure permission before establishing electronic reserves or creating course packs. Sometimes a historian will circulate a draft of a paper with the notation that it is not to be quoted or cited without the author's permission. It would show scholarly courtesy to comply. But none of these admonitions have the force of law unless you have agreed to them. If you do, enforcement of the agreement is not a matter of copyright but of contract.

What Is Protected by Copyright?

Copyright protects the author's right to reproduce and distribute her creative expressions. Because it originated with the advent of the printing press, copyright originally covered work that appeared in print. It has since expanded to cover creative expressions that don't necessarily appear in print—giving copyright owners the exclusive right to reproduce art works; perform dramas, musical works, and dances; display motion pictures; and distribute recordings. Computer programs are protected much like any other written expression. You have no copyright in statements you make in an ordinary conversation, unless the conversation is transcribed and you have expressly marked off the statement and indicated you want to reserve the right to publish it.

The law does not yet protect websites as a separate form of expression. It protects the program that formats a website as if it were text; it protects original creative text on the website as it does similar creative expressions in hard copy; it protects original graphics, photographs, and illustrations on a website as if they appeared separately in print; and it protects original music as if it appeared separately on a "phonorecording" (defined below). In many cases it will protect the selection of items for inclusion on a website from duplication. But if individual items on a website are not otherwise entitled to copyright protection, they will not secure it simply because they are part of a website.

Both graphic characters like Donald Duck and fictional literary characters like Rhett Butler are protected by copyright as long as they are fleshed out enough to take on specific identifiable characteristics. An artist cannot prevent someone from drawing a generic cat simply because he has drawn one first. Nor did Margaret Mitchell secure a copyright in all romantic Reconstruction-era scalawags, only in ones indistinguishable from Rhett Butler.

The main exclusive rights specified in the copyright statute are to:

(1) make copies

(2) prepare derivative works

(3) distribute copies to the public

(4) perform the work publicly

(5) display the work publicly[8]

"Derivatives" include edited versions of the original, translations, updated editions, and new works using the same fictional characters as the original. Creators have the same exclusive right to copy, distribute, display, and perform derivatives as they do original work. But a work that transforms the original into something new—for example, a parody or satire—is not a derivative but a new work, entitled to its own copyright.

To receive copyright protection, the creation must be fixed in some "tangible medium"—either a "copy" or a "phonorecord." The latter is a material object on which sounds are fixed—an audio cassette or a tape recording, for instance—separately from any connection to visuals. "Copies" are any other material objects on which works can be fixed and from which they can be communicated—from paper or canvas to videotapes, film, or ROM (permanent memory) chips in computers. You may reserve your rights to a conversation only if someone has recorded it. A broadcast or transmission does not "fix" a performance or event. Once the broadcast is over, the record is gone. The same is true if a student transmits your lecture to a friend over a cell phone. A broadcast is "fixed" if it is simultaneously taped, as nearly all commercial broadcasts are. E-mails and blogs are "fixed" if they are stored on a server or in a computer's permanent memory; similarly, your digitally transmitted lecture will be "fixed" only if it is downloaded and saved.

You have no copyright in a statement made orally in class, or extemporaneously at a conference, no matter how original and beautifully phrased, unless you or someone else has recorded it on tape, digitally, or in some other way that has "fixed" it. Therefore the student who tapes or makes a digital copy of your lecture has not infringed a copyright in your words, as they were not fixed in a tangible medium before she recorded them. This creates an ambiguous situation with regard to copyright. Musicians have secured special legislation to protect themselves from unauthorized taping and distribution of their otherwise unfixed performances.[9] No such "bootlegging" provision protects historians' unrecorded lectures. The student who has recorded your lecture without your permission owns the physical tape or the file in her digital camera. But she probably cannot use either one to circulate or distribute your words. Having been fixed, you have a copyright in them that she cannot infringe. If another scholar adapts your unfixed, oral exposition to his own use, scholarly courtesy requires that he acknowledge your creativity and perhaps even ask your permission. If he adapts too much of your oral, unfixed statement without attribution, he may be plagiarizing your work. But he won't have infringed your copyright.

Many copyrighted sources are now available online. Downloading them is the same as copying them. Posting them on one's own website infringes the copyright owner's exclusive right to display her work; it also may be considered distribution and thus infringe the copyright owner's exclusive right to distribute her work. If a library has acquired a license to display an electronic database consisting of copyrighted work, the database's owner will often specify the conditions of its use, including limits on downloading and copying. Such licenses usually will include permission to download and copy for personal research purposes. But with regard to works found through ordinary browsing, one should assume that sources created after 1923 are protected by copyright. Of course, when website owners are themselves the authors of the items they post, they can dedicate them to the public. The Creative Commons is a nonprofit organization that urges creators to do so and provides sample licenses waiving some or all rights (**http://creativecommons.org**).

The law gives copyright owners exclusive rights only to *public* distribution (including distribution through photocopying and downloading), display, and performance. Thus, if a historian writes a particularly evocative paragraph about some historical event, she can't prevent someone else from repeating it to a few others in a private setting, or from copying it for private use. Furthermore, there are exceptions to copyright protections that permit limited public use of a work for the purpose of criticism, scholarship, teaching, and news reporting. These exceptions began as judicial limitations on copyright, but they are now incorporated into the statutes and therefore are sometimes called "statutory exemptions." Congress has added other exemptions to copyright liability to protect nonprofit libraries and education. It has also excluded some work from copyright protection entirely—particularly work created by the United States government, such as the *Congressional Record*, the reports of cases decided by federal courts or administrative tribunals, and similar government publications.

Copyright only applies to the way one has expressed her insights or artistic vision, or the way in which she has transmitted her information. Sometimes that expression is not in the form of language, as it usually is for historians. It may be in the form of a painting or sculpture, a dance or other performance. It may even be in the creative decisions made when selecting or arranging documents or essays to appear in a compilation.

Owning a copyright does not give a historian or anyone else an exclusive property right to the information she transmits, no matter how unknown it was before she dug it out of the archives, or how hard she worked to find it.

It does not establish an exclusive property right in an idea, no matter how creative and innovative. If an idea or discovery has practical applications, one can secure the exclusive right to those applications by getting a *patent*. One cannot do it through copyright. It is the "expressive content"—the way in which an idea or information is communicated, not the idea or information itself—that copyright protects. Courts have held this to be particularly true of historical works. An important 1980 opinion put it this way: "[T]he scope of copyright in historical accounts is narrow indeed, embracing no more than the author's original expression of particular facts and theories."[10]

Whether a student infringes copyright by circulating her notes of your lecture—or selling them to a commercial provider of class notes—is a thorny question (assuming you have fixed the lectures in some medium in the first place). She has infringed if she has copied your words verbatim or paraphrased them closely. In that case, she has reproduced your creative expression. Both she and a commercial distributor would be liable for the infringement. But if her notes are only a report of what you said, she may not have infringed on your copyright, because the law protects your expression rather than the information or ideas that you convey. The issue might turn on how similar her language is to yours and how closely she followed your lecture's structure and organization.

Some universities have tried to bar the thriving business of selling class notes on the Internet and in course packets through student codes of conduct. University counsel have wisely advised lecturers to modify their syllabi to include statements reserving copyrights in classroom materials and withholding permission to make any commercial use of them.[11] Such statements do not themselves establish whether the distribution of student lecture notes are infringements, but someone who appropriates another's work may be liable to other kinds of civil actions. California has dealt with the problem by providing legal redress for appropriation of lectures or performances without permission.

In recent years Congress has augmented copyright laws by making it illegal to break the encryptions movie and television distributors and others have developed to foil copyright pirates.[12] The breadth of protection the law now gives owners of copyrights in these materials exceeds the traditional boundaries of copyright, and the effect has been to limit the rights traditionally given users.

Names, titles, common symbols, brief phrases, slogans, and *bon mots* are not protected by copyright, no matter how creative and original. In the review of a superficial book, you may ask, "Where's the beef?" without worrying about a lawsuit. However, don't be so free with words that have likely been registered as a *trademark*, another form of intellectual property protection. Advertising slogans can secure or earn trademark protection. So can titles of journals and magazines. You'll be in trouble if you decide to publish your own *American Historical Review*, but not because you have violated the AHA's copyright.

Beyond actual words, "expressive content" may include the substantive organization of a work and the way themes are developed and presented. One's work may violate copyright if it imitates the concept and feel of the original, not only in the ideas presented—these are not subject to copyright—but by the way it is organized, the similarity of the sources chosen and the way they are used, the events cited, and the context in which they are placed. A clear appropriation of another's written work, therefore, may be a violation of copyright even without the use of identical language. But it is very hard to prove such cases, and most efforts to do so fail. Since histories and biographies by their nature stress similar events, describe similar characters, and use similar sources, only rarely will a historian be able to prove a copyright infringement without demonstrating that his words themselves were copied. Presenting another historian's information or ideas as if they were one's own, without appropriating the language, organization, development, or presentation of the original, may make one guilty of *plagiarism* or a violation of professional standards, but it is not an infringement of copyright.

Moreover, if expressive content and an idea are so closely linked that one can only communicate the idea in one way, the expression is not protected by copyright. The expression and the factual content have "merged," as analysts say. Suppose you have established a list of the most important members of the Civil War Congress, using some criteria you have developed; it is unlikely that copyright will stop a succeeding scholar from reprinting the same list, especially if she provides appropriate scholarly attribution. There is simply no other way of expressing the uncopyrightable *idea* that these were the most important congressmen according to your criteria. (If she does not give you proper credit, a judge might well bend over backward to find an infringement. There is a lot of play in the application of copyright law; its limits are not a license to steal.)

On the other hand, a historian or other creator *is* expressing a protected idea when she compiles an anthology of primary and secondary sources for use in her own class or for sale to others. Her copyright is not in the sources themselves. The primary sources may no longer be protected by copyright—that is, they may be in the "public domain," a term explained in more detail below. The copyright in the secondary sources may still belong to the original author or his publisher (in which case the compiler must have secured permission to reproduce them). The compiler has a copyright only in the decisions she has made to select those sources; in the way she has organized them; and of course in any original comments she has made about them. Other teachers or publishers may not simply reproduce the anthology and distribute it, even after excising all additional comments. The same is true if a historian publishes a collection of original essays by his colleagues. The anthology's editor has a copyright in the selection he has made. Even if every single one of the authors gave permission, a new editor could not simply reproduce the collection. The same principle will protect the selection of material posted on a website. If you have chosen a number of old cartoons to illuminate the issues of the Gilded Age period of American history, for example, a colleague cannot simply download and transfer those cartoons to her own website. You don't have a copyright in the individual cartoons, but you do have a copyright in your selection. Of course, the universe of cartoons from which you drew must be large enough to make your selection a creative process. You could not put the only five cartoons published about a particular subject on your website and then claim no one else had a right to do the same thing.

Finally, to qualify for copyright protection, an expression must be original (not appropriated from someone else) and creative. Judges have interpreted even the most minimally creative and original expressions to qualify for protection. But a complete list of something organized alphabetically or chronologically—say, a telephone white pages—is not creative or original enough to gain copyright protection. A selective list or one organized on some more creative basis—say, the yellow pages—may qualify for protection, because the author has had to establish the criteria for selection and organization, much as do authors of the anthologies and collections described above.

If the owner of the copyright in a work permits it to be edited, the editor will have a copyright in the new version, while the original copyright holder retains the copyright in the original. Even if the original was in the public domain, an edited version will merit copyright protection, because the decisions about what to omit and what to include are creative.

Simple photographs of art work, newspaper cartoons, or book pages do not show enough creativity or originality to merit copyright protection. If the item photographed is not protected by copyright, one may use the photograph of it as one wishes. Likewise, one cannot secure a copyright merely by publishing the previously unpublished correspondence of a historical figure. If the originals are no longer protected by copyright—that is, if they are in the public domain—you may quote them in part or in their entirety from the newly published edition. Of course, your citation should indicate that fact, but this is a scholarly convention rather than a matter of copyright, The same is true of digital copies. The fact that someone took the trouble to scan and digitize the original does not give her a copyright in the facsimile. You may download and distribute it. This is why commercial image databases do not make good quality digital reproductions available on their sites unless users agree to pay for them and abide by conditions on further distribution. These conditions are a matter of contract, not copyright.

However, a photograph or digital reproduction that demonstrates creativity or originality by altering the original in some way does receive copyright protection. To use it you will need to secure permission, unless you want to use it in a way that the law says is not an infringement. Likewise, the editor of a published edition of previously unpublished correspondence or other material now in the public domain has a copyright in her introductory notes, her annotations, and any other original material she has added. If she has abridged the letters, she has a copyright in her abridgement. If she has selected letters for publication out of a larger number, one cannot take the same letters and republish them with one's own introductions and annotations. As a matter both of copyright law and professional ethics, one had best make one's own selections. Significant overlap is understandable as a matter of historical significance; near duplication is less so; complete reduplication is an infringement.

"Creators" and "creations" are loose terms that sound as if only something special is entitled to copyright protection. But the breadth of copyright means that, subject to legal exceptions, almost anything that shows even the slightest spark of creativity and originality is entitled to protection as soon as it is fixed in some tangible means of expression. Thus nearly everyone is a "creator," and nearly everything that we write down, draw, record on tape, film, or store in computer memory is a "creation" protected by copyright. We have copyrights in our published research, our syllabi, our research and lecture notes, the outlines of our public presentations, the reading lists we have provided students, and the e-mails we have sent friends. We own the copyright in our conference presentations from the moment they were audio- or videotaped, unless we read them from text, in which case we owned the copyright in the presentations from the time we wrote them down. We have copyrights in the notes we have stored on our computer or written on an index card, in drafts of undelivered lectures, exam questions we never used; we own the copyright to anything of minimal creativity and originality that we have written down or stored on a hard disk. We may transfer our rights to publishers, to journals, to conference organizers, or to anyone else we choose.

WEBSITES AND COPYRIGHT

Copyright does not protect websites as a single entity. It protects the format by protecting the computer program that created it, but the content is protected according to the same rules that would apply to it in a hard copy or in a phonorecord. Merely digitizing the content, without further significant alteration, does not establish a copyright in the digitized version. The general rule is that copyright does not protect mere effort, no matter how difficult.[13] If the website owner has secured permission to post copyrighted material, any infringement will be of the original owner's rights, not those of the website owner.

However, the website owner has a copyright in the selections made, just like the author of any compilation. Another historian cannot simply duplicate his website, any more than she could duplicate the selections included in a class source reader. Consider again the example of a historian who has digitized a group of cartoons published in the nineteenth century and posted them on a website, along with commentary putting them in context. Eliminating the historian's original text and selecting some of the cartoons for a site of one's own will not violate copyright. Nor would including the cartoons in a larger selection. Copyright protection for the cartoons themselves has expired (as explained below, they are in the "public domain"). What a historian cannot do is simply download all the cartoons from one website onto another, with no substantial additions or subtractions.

OWNERSHIP OF COPYRIGHT

Usually the author of a creative expression initially owns the copyright. So students own the copyright to their own papers, tests, and anything else prepared for class. If a faculty member wants to secure the right to make copies for instructional purposes, she should ask permission or state in the syllabus that such permission is assumed unless a student objects. Retaining a single photocopy for grading purposes after handing back the original would be a "fair use," a concept discussed below. Distributing copies to other students without permission, even for educational purposes, would be a closer call.

But the author of a creative expression does not always own the initial copyright. Unless an agreement specifies otherwise, the copyright in a "work made for hire" by an employee in the course of her employment is normally owned by the employer. If certain, limited kinds of creative works are specially commissioned, they may be owned by the person or entity that commissioned them.

The law is not clear about whether work produced by faculty is "work made for hire" and therefore owned by the colleges and universities that employ them. Before the overhaul of the copyright statute in 1976, judges had created a clear "teacher's exception" to its work-made-for-hire provisions. But the 1976 act did not explicitly incorporate this exception. The language of the law appears to make faculty work prepared within the scope of academic employment the property of employers. But no court has yet decided that the failure to mention the "teacher's exception" abrogated it, and some cases have implied that it may survive.[14] Nonetheless, the trend appears to be against maintaining the exception as a legal rule and towards treating it merely as a custom subject to alteration by colleges and universities.

In the absence of an agreement between administrators and faculty, courts might hold that colleges and universities own the copyrights to faculty members' creative work, especially if publication or artistic production is a condition of employment and promotion. In such a case, the question would become whether a particular work was created within the scope of employment. Even if prepared at home, instructional materials intended for use in one's own classes would almost certainly be considered works made for hire. Research publications in the field one teaches might be considered works made for hire as well. Because historians at universities do not work fixed hours, it is quite difficult to insist that one's work has been prepared on one's own time and should not be considered a work made for hire.

Few, if any, college administrations have yet laid claim to the creative work of their arts, humanities, and social science faculties. Most research-oriented academic institutions have detailed policies governing the relationship between the institution, its faculty, and the fruits of their research. Generally, these policies either recognize faculty members' full ownership of copyrights in literary and artistic productions, or they claim ownership but then cede it away. But increased financial pressure has led universities to consider clarifying their rules in order to capitalize on the creative work of their faculties. Tensions have developed especially with regard to the ownership of copyright in online courses. Historians would be wise to confirm the situation in their own institutions.[15] They would be even wiser to negotiate agreements through collective bargaining, or to establish them through the collective governance procedures established at most universities.

The working hours of history teachers at secondary schools and of public historians are more clearly defined. Yet it is not always clear that a work prepared on one's own time, away from the office, is one's own. Location and time of creation are only two considerations in deciding whether work was created in the course of employment. Other considerations include whether one used the employer's staff or equipment, whether one used information gathered as part of one's employment, whether the creation was related to work projects, and whether it was in part designed to serve the employer's interests. If the creation is prepared within the scope of employment according to these criteria, it is a work for hire. If a public historian prepares a study related to the field in which he is engaged at work, it may be considered a work for hire, especially if he uses sources gathered on the job. On the other hand, if a historian prepares a study in a different field than the one in which he is employed, the copyright belongs to him.

Historians will sometimes prepare work for others. We may be paid honoraria for delivering lectures at public gatherings, or for contributing an essay to a volume on some subject related to our fields. In such cases we ordinarily are independent contractors, and the copyright in what we prepare belongs to us, unless the agreement specifies differently. The law severely limits what may be considered work for hire when prepared by an independent contractor, and it requires the concession to be in writing. A contribution to a collective work may be undertaken by an independent contractor as a work for hire. A historian might enter contracts to prepare compilations, instructional texts, tests, and supplementary materials as works made for hire. With few other exceptions, the copyright in commissioned work belongs to the historian who prepared it. Even when we are asked to curate exhibitions at museums or prepare corporate histories, the copyright belongs to us in the absence of a contract specifying the contrary.

However, circumstances may indicate that we were in fact employees rather than independent contractors; if so, our creations will be works made for hire. Self-employed historians, particularly, should be aware of this possibility. These circumstances include the degree of control whoever has hired the work has over its production, their control over our hours, whether we prepare the work on their premises and with their equipment, whether they have the right to add further duties, the degree of independent skill the task requires, how we are paid, whether payment includes employee benefits, and whether the work is similar to what the hirer usually produces (for example, museums produce exhibits; automobile manufacturers do not normally produce corporate histories). Where there appears to be some ambiguity, a historian should make sure that ownership of copyright is clarified in the agreement to undertake the task.

Like any other property, a copyright is transferable. An author can delegate the right to distribute her work to someone else, and usually does—to a book or journal publisher. One might transfer all future distribution rights of every kind to a publisher, or one might assign some rights to one party, others to another, and keep some rights for oneself. Publishers often seek to secure all present and future rights in a work, in every technology now existing or to be invented in the future. The broader the language delegating rights, the more a court may be inclined to decide a dispute in the publisher's favor. In an age of dynamic change in information media, consider the wisdom of agreeing to a blanket transfer of rights. Historians should understand that when they transfer all their copyrights to publishers, the publisher can distribute an edited version of the historian's work or authorize someone else to do so.

THE HISTORIAN AND "MORAL RIGHTS"

American copyright law does not reserve a "moral right" in creators—excepting visual artists—to restrict where and how their work can be distributed or altered by the owner of its copyright. A historian who transfers all rights to a publisher gives up any control over how her work may be altered and where it may be used in the United States. However, most nations have agreed to enforce the "moral rights" secured by the Berne Convention, and therefore American historians can exert moral rights over their publishers' use of their work abroad.

Because American copyright law does not recognize moral rights, there are limits to how much you can control the use of your work by others. You cannot prevent someone from making fair use of your work simply because you do not like the purpose or the people involved. Nor can you prevent its use merely to maintain your privacy. You have more control over the use of your unpublished work, because the law recognizes your right to decide when and how to first publish it. But with regard to published work, American copyright law protects economic rather than moral rights.

Nonetheless, copyright owners can try to stop objectionable uses of their work. Although the purpose of copyright is to protect economic interests, a copyright owner's motive for challenging a use is irrelevant to the outcome of the case. If the criteria that determine fair use are not met, the copyright has been infringed, the use can be enjoined, and the infringer can be made to pay damages.

THE PUBLIC DOMAIN

Creations not protected by copyright are in the "public domain." Creative expressions come into the public domain for one of four reasons: (1) they were never entitled to copyright protection in the first place, (2) the copyright owner failed to follow rules governing copyright before revised laws went into effect in 1978, (3) the owner of the copyright decided to place it in the public domain, dedicating it to public use, or (4) the copyright term has expired.

Until the United States modified its copyright laws to conform to the Berne Convention in 1989, work published without a copyright notice immediately went into the public domain, although the 1976 law made it possible to remedy the omission. Now eligible work is protected as soon as it is fixed in a tangible medium. Expressions not eligible for protection—names, titles, slogans, common symbols, expressions that have too little original, creative content—are in the public domain and free for public use, unless they are entitled to trademark protection. What the U.S. Copyright Office calls "edicts" of government—including legislation, ordinances, judicial opinions, and administrative rulings—whether federal, state, or local, are in the public domain as soon as they are released. So are all other *federal* government records and works created by federal government officers and employees in the course of their jobs. The republication and electronic postings of such government documents by private companies or individuals does not alter the status of the underlying material. Only newly added material—introductions, annotations, etc.—are protected by copyright. As long as they exclude such editorial additions, historians may download the documents, display them on their own websites or on class websites, photocopy their published versions, and distribute them in class.

Of particular importance to historians, individual federal agencies decide whether works prepared under contracts and grants receive copyright protection or go directly into the public domain as government-generated records. The National Endowment for the Humanities explicitly states that recipients of its financial support may copyright resulting work. Any historian securing a government grant or contract to support her research or publication should determine the policy of the granting agency.

The law is different with regard to state and local government records and publications—other than those that qualify as "edicts" of government—because the copyright statute exempts only *federal* documents and publications from protection. Most states have established no rule regarding the materials they generate. A historian seeking to use such materials would have to check with the agency sponsoring the publication to discover its rules. In Ohio, for instance, the informal rule seems to be that official publications of state employees are freely available for public use unless specifically withheld.

States may dedicate their copyrights to the public, and so may any other copyright owner. There is a growing disposition among scientists and scholars to do this—to provide "open access" to articles and working papers. Material posted on the Internet sometimes is accompanied by a dedication of rights to the public. Historians should bear in mind, however, that too broad a dedication of rights may grant the public blanket permission to edit and make use of one's work in dismaying ways. Such dedications should be worded carefully.

As copyright owners become more vigilant about their rights, historians will have to think harder about whether their use of copyrighted material qualifies as fair use and is therefore exempt from the general rule that owners have the sole right to distribute and adapt their work. This will often be difficult to determine. When work in the public domain can serve the historian's purpose, choosing it over work under copyright protection can avoid a host of problems.

Most importantly, copyright runs only for a fixed time. When that time is exhausted, the copyrighted work enters the public domain and is freely available to all. It can be republished, redistributed, put online, and excerpted in sourcebooks. Music in the public domain can be performed, recorded, and used as background in documentaries. (However, specific recorded performances may still be protected by copyright, long after the music itself has come into the public domain.) The words Abraham Lincoln uttered in the Lincoln-Douglas Debates are no longer protected by copyright, but a new recorded reading of them would be from the date of its creation.

Although many cartoons, works of arts, and photographs are in the public domain because their copyright terms have run out, commercial organizations specializing in granting licenses and permission for the use of creative work include them on their databases. Historians may find these commercial databases useful for finding old images to use in teaching, research, or publication. Some of the databases include images even of ephemera like broadsides and posters. Historians will have to pay for downloading good quality images from these databases, even if they are in the public domain, and will be bound to observe license agreements accompanying the transaction.

The owners of image databases provide thumbnail versions of the images they license to customers. Clicking on the thumbnail images leads to the high-quality version users can download for a fee. Generally, the database owners do not require potential customers to enter into license agreements merely to peruse the thumbnails. If the thumbnails are of images in the public domain, the thumbnails themselves can be downloaded and reproduced if a low-quality image will serve the historian's purpose. (To discourage this practice, some databases imprint their names on the thumbnail images.) Despite this fact, historians should first consult noncommercial databases that have posted thousands of high-quality images in the public domain, such as the Library of Congress's *An American Time Capsule* (**http://memory. loc.gov/ammem/rbpehtml**). Libraries, museums, and historical societies are putting more and more documents, ephemera, and photographs online.

THE "FIRST-SALE" PRINCIPLE

Ownership of a copyright and ownership of the tangible copyrighted item—a book or a painting, for example—are two different things. With regard to the tangible item, copyright protects only the right of "first sale." That is, the copyright owner controls only the initial sale of his book, painting, sculpture, photograph, or other tangible item, not its subsequent disposal. With some exceptions to protect movies, sound recordings, and computer software, the buyer has the right to display, lend, or dispose of the work in any way she wishes. The author cannot stop the resale of a purchased copy, nor prevent a public or corporate library from lending copies it has acquired. Neither can a painter or sculptor stop a museum from displaying her work or control its subsequent sale. An architect cannot stop the sale of his building, nor can a movie distributor prevent one from reselling a purchased DVD. However, owning a book does not free you to put on a public reading; nor does owning the recording of a movie or an album, or the script of a play, mean you can perform it publicly.

In general, the purchaser of a copyrighted work can lend it out, even charging the borrower. The only exceptions to this rule are limits on the right to lend computer software and sound recordings in any medium, because it is so easy for the borrower to make a personal copy and return the borrowed one. A borrowed book does not present the same threat to copyright owners. Therefore, while the Copyright Act generally bars purchasers from lending sound recordings and computer programs for "commercial advantage," it does not impose a similar restriction on lending books or even videotapes or DVDs.

There are exceptions to the ban on lending sound recordings and computer software that are important for historians and other academics: Nonprofit libraries are permitted to lend them if they include a copyright warning on the packaging. Nonprofit educational institutions are allowed to transfer possession of computer programs they have purchased to students, faculty, staff, and other nonprofit educational institutions. However, none of these concessions means that we can make copies of the records or computer programs for later use.

While the purchaser has broad rights to use and dispose of a particular copy of a work, acquiring a book, journal, painting, or other creative product does not transfer the copyright to the buyer. The collector cannot distribute reproductions of his artworks; the owner of a building cannot authorize another builder to duplicate it. Nor could the purchaser of a history book distribute photocopies of the whole work or a substantial part of it. For the same reason, a teacher cannot photocopy substantial portions of books and articles he owns and distribute them to students, unless he secures permission from the copyright owners. Nor can he scan the material and post it on a class website.

Of special interest to historians, the writer retains the copyright in a letter sent to a correspondent. The recipient owns the physical letter and can display it, send it along to an acquaintance, or sell it to a dealer in manuscripts. But unless he gets permission, the recipient cannot reprint or publish it, or authorize others to do so. If the recipient ultimately donates her papers to a library or archive, she cannot transfer the copyright to anything but the material she herself has written. Likewise, the writer or his heirs own the copyright in an unpublished diary or any other unpublished manuscript. If an unpublished manuscript or a writer's correspondence comes into the hands of a historical society, the copyright does not come with it. Unless the work has passed into the public domain, or the author or his heirs have transferred it to the repository, the copyright remains theirs.

A manuscript repository may require that you secure its permission to make use of an item in its possession. After all, it owns the tangible item, even if it doesn't own the copyright, and one of the rights of ownership in any property is to set conditions for access to it. You may have to secure the institution's consent before quoting the item in a publication, posting it on the Internet, or using it as an illustration in a PowerPoint display. This agreement may be legally enforceable as a matter of contract, but copyright law has nothing to do with it.

DURATION OF COPYRIGHT

The U.S. Constitution authorizes Congress to protect the exclusive rights of creators to their creations "for limited Times" in order "to promote the Progress of Science and useful Arts." So everything goes out of copyright and enters the public domain sooner or later. The limited duration for which works receive copyright protection is particularly important to historians, who are more likely than most to utilize older materials. Before the wholesale revision of 1976, whether a work received copyright protection at all, and for how long, depended on a variety of factors. The 1976 act was designed to simplify all this.[16] Any eligible work created on or after January 1, 1978, receives copyright protection as soon as it is created, whether it is published or not. Protection continues through the life of the creator or of the longest-living joint creator, plus seventy years. Works created for hire are protected for 95 years after their first publication or 120 years from their creation, whichever is shorter. Works published anonymously or under a pseudonym receive these terms of protection as well, since one cannot determine the date of the creator's death. In all cases, copyright protection ends on the last day of the relevant year; if the author of a work completed in 1978 died in 2000, for example, the work's copyright protection would end on December 31, 2070, and it would come into the public domain in 2071.

These lengthy terms of copyright protection, extended in part to conform to the international standard set by the Berne Convention, have dismayed many librarians, scholars, and consumer advocates. After all, the first copyright law, passed by the nation's founders in 1790, provided for only fourteen years of protection, renewable for another fourteen. Until the Copyright Act of 1976 went into effect in 1978, the law provided protection for only twenty-eight years, renewable for another twenty-eight. Critics challenged the most recent update, arguing that it extended copyright terms beyond the "limited" time permitted by the Constitution, thus promoting monopoly rather than creativity. The case went all the way to the Supreme Court, which deferred to congressional authority.[17] Under the present law, if a graduate student publishes her first book at the age of twenty-five, it might be protected for 130 years or more. Her freshman compositions will be protected even longer. Unpublished letters and manuscripts receive the same life-plus-seventy-years protection, even if written before 1978.

While the Copyright Act of 1976 eventually will simplify the rules governing the term of copyright, it certainly has not done so in the short run, because it gave various terms of protection to work published before 1978. If a work had already entered the public domain, the 1976 act did not bring it back under copyright protection, except in a very few cases.[18] Under the convoluted provisions of the act and later amendments, copyright protection has expired for all work published before 1923. Work published after 1924 may have come into the public domain for a variety of reasons. But further term extensions mean that no more published work will enter the public domain until 2019.

The situation is different for unpublished materials. Work that was unpublished as of 1976, but then published before 2003, will have copyright protection until 2047 or seventy years after the death of the creator, whichever comes later. Copyrights in work that was not published by 2003 expire seventy years after the creator's death. The unpublished work of creators who died in 1940 came into the public domain in 2011. The unpublished work of those who died in 1941 will come into the public domain in 2012, and so on. Thus, no private, unpublished letter written by Eleanor Roosevelt, who died in 1962, will enter the public domain until 2033. Those published before the end of 2003 won't enter the public domain until 2047.

The Appendix (starting on page 53) discusses the duration of copyright for works published since 1923 and provides a chart delineating the copyright status of all work that has been eligible for its protection.

LIMITS ON COPYRIGHT
FOR THE BENEFIT OF USERS

The most widely accepted justification for copyright is that it promotes creativity and the production of knowledge by providing an incentive to creators. But too rigid protection of copyrighted works might instead inhibit creativity by making it impossible or inordinately expensive to build upon the work of others or to teach. Therefore judges established limits and exemptions that have been incorporated into the copyright statutes themselves. Congress has also established new exemptions and reformulated old ones in response to requests from educational institutions, teachers, and librarians.

CLASSROOM EXEMPTIONS

Congress has consistently tried to protect educational activities from being severely circumscribed by copyright law. In addition to including education among the purposes for which one can make fair use of a copyrighted work, the copyright statute exempts a variety of classroom activities from copyright restrictions. Instructors have the same right as every other owner of a copyrighted work to display it, and may exhibit their copy of a book, poster, photograph, or painting in the classroom. But owners do not have the same right to "perform" a work that they have to display it. Thus one cannot stage a play simply because one owns a copy of the script, perform music simply because one owns a copy of the sheet music, read from a book because one owns a copy, nor show a movie simply because one owns the DVD. However, Congress has made an exception for face-to-face classroom instruction, and students and teachers can do all these things in a traditional classroom setting.

The Copyright Office, which has generally been sympathetic to the interests of copyright owners, has also taken small steps to promote education. For example, it has exempted scholars and teachers from the provision making it illegal to break encryptions on movies and other digitized material so that they may use small portions for education or criticism.[19] This rule has not stopped media companies from trying to prevent educators from making fair use of their encrypted digital materials, but at least they won't go to jail for doing so.

Congress has also enacted a special revision to the copyright laws: the Technology, Education, and Copyright Harmonization (or TEACH) Act. This enables nonprofit, accredited colleges and universities to provide distance education analogous to classroom teaching. The law was carefully crafted to prevent wholesale scanning and transmission of copyrighted work, and to protect products created specifically for the educational market. In order to take advantage of it colleges and universities must take a variety of steps, including the dissemination of formal copyright policies to faculty, students, and other staff. Access must be limited to students enrolled in a class "mediated" by an instructor, and transmissions of copyrighted materials cannot be retained after use in a class session. Institutions must take steps to prevent students from further disseminating copyrighted materials. If these and other requirements are met, instructors may make almost the same use of materials over the Internet that they can in their classrooms.

Almost. The law explicitly bars the transmission of works specially designed to be marketed for performance or display in classrooms. The law does not authorize the transmission, for example, of online databases designed for classroom use or educational videos and compact discs marketed to instructors.

The provisions of the TEACH Act may have applications beyond organized distance learning. Some universities are relying on its provisions to stream instructional materials on university-owned CDs directly to students, over the objections of distributors, who want to charge a licensing fee for such uses. This practice might replace or augment electronic reserves or class websites. If the courts uphold such applications of the TEACH Act, our institutions will have to meet the law's requirements and establish a formal process for electronic transmissions. In the meantime, instructors will have to rely on the doctrine of fair use to justify appropriate transmissions of copyrighted materials to their students.

Library Exemptions and the Historian

If inflexibly applied, copyright law would interpose insuperable barriers to the services libraries have come to provide their patrons. The customary use of photocopiers would infringe copyrights, making both the patron and the library liable for damages. Students could not photocopy copyrighted material held on a reserve shelf. Photocopies of journal articles could not be sent through interlibrary loan. Libraries could not lend sound recordings. To avoid destroying the benefits libraries afford society, the copyright statute exempts a number of activities in libraries and archives from being treated as infringements, while at the same time trying to protect the interests of copyright owners.[20] Most of these exemptions apply only to nonprofit libraries and archives that are open to the public or to researchers unaffiliated with the library or its sponsoring institution. No library, even a nonprofit one, can utilize these exemptions for commercial advantage.

Some of the exemptions help libraries maintain, protect, and preserve their collections. Some enable them to provide services that might otherwise make them liable for distributing copyrighted work. The exemptions also protect libraries from "contributory liability" for the actions of their patrons. Some are crucial to historians as researchers and teachers. The exemptions permit a library to copy limited portions of a copyrighted work in its collection to send through interlibrary loan. Interlibrary loan copies and copies made onsite must be for private study, scholarship, or research, and they must become the property of the patron. The works may be digitally scanned rather than photocopied. But the library cannot make a digital copy of the work for patrons to download, unless it removes the digital copy from its hard drive or server immediately after the patron downloads his copy. The exemption permits a library to make a permanent digital reproduction of a copyrighted work only for preserving and maintaining collections, not for making further copies. Of course, a library may purchase a digital copy of a work, in which case it can make copies for patrons within the same limits specified for any other copying. Alternatively, it may license digital collections of works with provisions for downloading and copying.

The copying exemption is limited to protect copyright owners. It does not apply to music, pictures, photographs, graphics, motion pictures or other audiovisuals, except for news reports, unless they are adjuncts to books and articles. It permits a library to provide patrons with only one copy of an article, a chapter in a collection of essays or other collected work, or a small portion of a book or play. It authorizes a library to copy an entire work, but only if it cannot otherwise be obtained for a reasonable price. Each instance of copying must be isolated and unrelated to other copying.

The rules ease a little with regard to published works in the last twenty years of copyright protection. If the work is no longer being exploited commercially and is unavailable at a reasonable price, nonprofit libraries can make hard or digital copies of any portion. They can display the work online, distribute it, or copy it, as long as the purpose is scholarship, research, or preservation. In other words, as long as they are no longer on the market, nonprofit libraries can treat printed work and nonmusical recordings in the last twenty years of their copyright term much as if they were in the public domain. Historians share the benefit, even though the law does not give us similar rights as individuals.

Rather than burdening their own employees with the task, most libraries provide photocopy machines that enable us to do our own copying. But the copying must be for the specified purposes of private study, scholarship, or research. And no matter who does the photocopying, the exemption applies primarily to print materials. To offer some bit of reassurance to copyright owners, libraries are required to display "prominently" a warning that photocopied materials may be protected by copyright.

These exemptions enable historians to put materials owned by the library on reserve and instruct students to photocopy portions of them. But the exemption does not immunize a library from liability if a teacher makes his own photocopies and puts them on the reserve shelf for circulation to students. Nor is a library exempt from liability if its employees know that a teacher is copying a work in order to distribute it to her students in class. The teacher's activities may constitute a fair use of the copyrighted material. If so, no liability will attach to anyone. But if the teacher exceeds the boundaries of fair use, both she and the library will be legally account-able. Nor does the exemption authorize an electronic reserve system, in which the library posts course material for students to download.

The copyright statute's explicit exemptions do not exhaust the services libraries can provide to patrons or the actions they might take to maintain their collections. Other services to historians—for example, replacing traditional reserve shelves with electronic reserves—might be deemed fair uses of copyrighted material. Likewise, one can make fair use of the pictures, graphics, and audiovisual materials that don't come under the explicit library exemptions. The exemptions provide what experts have analogized to a "safe harbor." If one stays within their limits and fulfills the requirements they impose, the library will be immune from copyright liability. If libraries go beyond the exemptions, they must defend their actions as fair use.

Despite Congress's effort to frame a relatively detailed provision regarding library exemptions, the law remains vague enough to make librarians nervous. To provide more definite guidance, a variety of groups have set out guidelines, some of which are the results of negotiation among librarians, publishers, and other interested parties. Such guidelines inform librarians what publishers— the dominant copyright owners—will consider acceptable. Although they establish only the minimum rights that libraries have with regard to photocopying, interlibrary loan, class reserves, and other subjects, many libraries adhere to them as if they established legal limits. They have been encouraged in this mistaken belief because Congress referred to the guidelines in reports and legislative histories accompanying the copyright statute. Moreover, judges have sometimes treated the guidelines as official interpretations of the law, despite explicit congressional language to the contrary.

THE HISTORIAN AND "FAIR USE"

Early in the history of American copyright law, judges ruled that certain uses of published works were not infringements of copyright. The Copyright Act of 1976 incorporated this doctrine of "fair use" into the statute itself, "for purposes such as criticism, comment, news reporting, teaching (including multiple copies for classroom use), scholarship, or research." After some confusion, Congress amended the law to make clear that the principle applied to unpublished as well as published work.[21] The statute also explicitly incorporated the criteria that courts had developed for determining whether a use was fair:

(1) the purpose and character of the use

(2) the nature of the copyrighted work

(3) the amount of the original used and its
   "substantiality" in relation to the work as a whole

(4) the effect of the use upon the potential market for
   the work and on its market value

Although the language did not explicitly limit the criteria to those listed, in practice courts now consider each criterion in turn before deciding whether, on balance, a use has been fair.

The doctrine of fair use limits the exclusive control that copyright gives historians and their publishers over the distribution of their work. We cannot object—at least not successfully—that reviewers are infringing our copyright when they briefly quote our work, whether they do so in hard copy or online. We cannot successfully claim an infringement on the part of scholars who quote us to bolster their own insights, nor can we object if a revisionist quotes us while challenging our conclusions. Teachers may make limited use of our work in their classes. Other scholars may photocopy some portions of our work as part of their own research. And we can do the same with theirs.

Historians have a special interest in the doctrine of fair use, both as researchers and teachers. In our research and writing, we rely and build upon the work of those who have gone before us. More than most, we utilize the actual words of our sources to support our arguments. As teachers, we distribute copies of primary and secondary sources to stimulate the historical imaginations of our students and to enable them to engage first-hand in debates over interpretation. But questions remain. How much use, and what sorts of uses, are fair, and how much and what sorts of uses constitute infringements? There are no hard and fast rules. One can be confident, for instance, that brief quotations in a book review are fair use. One can be confident that duplicating substantial portions of a competitor's textbook in our own is not. The problems arise in what lies in between. The uncertainty might discourage fair use of copyrighted material. Alternatively, it might encourage a historian to ignore the complexities and make decisions based on the likelihood of getting caught. Either course would be mistaken. Congress has encouraged educators to take advantage of the fair-use doctrine by eliminating statutory damages where educators and librarians make honest and reasonable mistakes.

If push comes to shove, what constitutes fair use in any specific case will be decided by judges in court. The difficulty is that one cannot predict with much certainty how judges will react to specific fact patterns beyond the most obvious. Judges consistently affirm that each claim of fair use must be considered on its own merits. This pattern of decision-making leaves few fixed rules to guide a historian who wants to copy a work in the course of her own research, quote it in her own publications, or convey it to students in her classes. In an effort to provide some certainty, publishers and educators have negotiated guidelines. These constitute "safe harbors" for teachers wishing to adhere to them, but they are minimum interpretations and therefore more restrictive than other, equally reasonable interpretations of the law.

Because there are no hard and fast rules, there is a tendency among analysts to think in terms of what a judge would decide in the case of a particular controversy. But this approach puts too great a constraint on the application of fair use. The tendency to avoid acts that might subject us to litigation is even more pronounced in lawyers paid to advise universities how to avoid liability. Although publishers and music and motion picture distributors have become more aggressive in fighting possible infringements, litigation remains unlikely unless an infringement is particularly widespread or egregious. The historian's obligation is to evaluate her rights fairly and honestly, helped by university guidelines and other aids, without letting an exaggerated fear of litigation determine her decisions. The law itself encourages reasonable decisions by mitigating damages against employees or agents of nonprofit educational institutions who "believed and had reasonable grounds for believing that his or her use of the copyrighted work was a fair use" under the criteria specified by the copyright statute.[22]

Judges tend to evaluate each criterion of fair use separately, limiting themselves somewhat artificially to the four criteria explicitly mentioned in the copyright statute. As a practical matter it is easiest for historians to do the same when considering whether a particular use would be fair. But the criteria are closely interrelated, and the factors are to be compared and balanced; it is not necessary for every factor to weigh on the side of fair use.

(1) *The purpose of the use.* The Copyright Act expressly states that criticism, comment, news reporting, teaching, scholarship, and research are among the purposes for which one may make use of another's copyrighted work without securing permission. However, employing a copyrighted work for these purposes does not of itself render the use fair. Other factors may outweigh the scholarly or educational purposes to which historians put copyrighted work.

Photocopying, downloading, saving, and printing a portion of a work in the service of one's own—with no commercial advantage accruing beyond the possibility of royalties sometime in the future—are the sorts of uses the law favors. So are the same activities for the purpose of broadening our personal knowledge, deepening our understanding of history as a discipline and practice, gaining insight into epistemology, or improving our teaching methods. The statutory library exemptions discussed above make clear that copying for such purposes is fair use by mandating that copies produced for patrons must become "the property of the user" for the purpose of "private study, scholarship, or research."[23]

The fair-use provision of the copyright statute states that to assess the nature of a use, one must consider "whether such use is of a commercial nature or is for nonprofit educational purposes." Given this either/or language, it is clear that noncommercial uses are more likely to be called fair than commercial ones, even if the commercial use is directly connected to research or education. Putting part of a copyrighted work on a class website, to be downloaded in a way that brings no income to the instructor, is more unmistakably fair use than including the same portion in an anthology intended for sale. So too is a study guide you prepare to help your students understand a supplementary reading assignment. But you probably could not publish and sell the same study guide and sell it commercially without permission from the owner of the copyright in the work being studied. Preparing such "derivative" works is a privilege the law reserves to the creator or those to whom he has assigned his rights. Even the educational purpose of the use, and the fact that the study guide is aimed at a different audience than was the original work, is unlikely to outweigh the copyright owner's right to control the commercial distribution of derivatives.

A work is not "of a commercial nature" simply because it makes money for its author and publisher. Briefly quoting a copyrighted work in a scholarly monograph, even one marketed at a high price by a university press, still serves a primarily nonprofit educational purpose. Its goal is more to transmit knowledge than to make a profit for either the author or publisher, at least if published in a typically small printing. Similar quotations in an unfootnoted historical blockbuster or bestselling textbook probably still constitute fair use, but not as certainly.

Using a copy shop to prepare a photocopied or digital classroom reader shifts the equation. The teacher is engaging in a nonprofit, educational use when she prepares material to go to the shop. But the shop is a commercial, for-profit business, and courts have come down hard against the argument that commercial photo-duplication qualifies as fair use. The copy shop will generally insist on securing permissions for the reproduction of copyright-ed work, rendering issues of fair use moot. If the teacher himself distrib-utes work to students—as photocopies, by posting the material on a class website, or by establishing electronic reserves through the library—and makes no profit out of the endeavor, all the criteria of fair use come into play. However, the instructor must take care to limit the distribution of materials to students enrolled in her class. She should post course materials on a website restricted through a password or other means, rather than simply post them on her own unrestricted website. Photocopied materials passed out in class should include a clear statement—preferably in the class syllabus—that they not be further copied and distributed.

A use that transforms the original into something substantially new— such as a parody, a sculpture used as the basis for an editorial cartoon, or the incorporation of newspaper articles into an artistic collage—is presumptively fair. These are creative works, and copyrights in them belong to their creators. Less complete "transformative uses" also tend to be ruled fair. When a historian quotes a source in his own published work, he has transformed it by placing it in a new historical context. Likewise, embedding a portion of a work in a webframe that explains its historical setting would be a transformative use. Taking characters from a copyrighted work and inserting them into a historical event to stimulate student interest might qualify as fair use, especially if—probably *only* if—no commercial advantage accrued to the historian or publisher. But the transformation would not be a fair use if the characters engaged in similar activities in the original, or if they regularly appear in a variety of contexts. If someone has published *Adventures of a Time-Traveling Boy*, don't set her characters in your own historical recreation, even if you distribute it for free and only to your own class. That goes in spades for your ingenious classroom handout *Mickey Mouse at the Alamo*.

The historian should consider the essential purpose to which she is putting a copyrighted work. Using a commercial work to serve a narrowly educational function unrelated to commerce has itself been held to be transformative. Using an excerpt from an Elvis Presley performance in class to illustrate the convergence of white rockabilly and African American rhythm and blues, or to demonstrate the effect of black popular culture on white society in the 1950s, clearly serves a nonprofit educational purpose different from that motivating the original creation and its commercial distribution. Using the same performance simply as background music for a series of PowerPoint slides about pop culture in the fifties does not serve an educational purpose so clearly. Unless it is made a more integral part of the presentation, the music merely makes the slide show more entertaining—the same purpose Elvis and his distributors had in the first place. Utilizing music completely unrelated to the subject of the slides probably does not serve an educational purpose at all. Even though it is associated with an educational activity, the purpose is more to entertain than instruct. An instructor must either secure permission or use the music in a way that underscores its educational purpose.

The spontaneity of the decision to use a work is also a consideration. If something has come up in class that makes the distribution of a copyrighted work particularly appropriate, the use is more likely fair than one long planned. Likewise, using a work year after year is less likely to be fair than using it once. This does not mean that the instructor must stop using a particularly effective excerpt from a copyrighted source. It is only one more factor to be considered among many.

An educational or scholarly use implies adherence to professional standards of conduct. When making fair use of another's work, one should always give scholarly credit to the author, and excerpt fairly from the original, without distortion. In the unlikely case of litigation, judges have been known to treat unscholarly conduct as inconsistent with a claim of educational or scholarly purpose.[24]

(2) *The nature of the copyrighted work.* As the *Mickey Mouse* example indicates, the nature of a copyrighted work may weigh against finding even a nonprofit scholarly or educational use to be fair. Legal precedent makes clear that use of material drawn from nonfiction work is more likely to be deemed fair than uses that draw from works of fiction, poetry, music, and the visual arts. However, the nature of historical research and education makes this distinction less relevant for historians than for other users. If the material is clearly put to an educational purpose—as would be distributing an excerpt from Ralph Ellison's *Invisible Man* (1952) to illustrate race relations in the 1940s—the fact that it is a novel rather than nonfiction should weigh only lightly, if at all, against considering the use fair. The fact that it is being put to a different purpose than the original, that only a small amount of the original is being used, and that the effect on the original's marketability is minimal will outweigh the fact that it is artistic rather than factual.

Indeed, instructors should use some factual works with caution. In preparing a teacher-distributed classroom reader or a website for an American history survey, it is less likely that reprinting part of a history textbook would qualify as fair use than would reproducing an excerpt from *Invisible Man.* A textbook is designed for classroom use, and photocopying it for a course reader duplicates the original's own nature and function. This makes questions of marketability and market value particularly relevant.

The availability of a published work is also relevant. One can feel freer to use a work that is out of print and difficult to secure than one that is commercially available at a reasonable price. This is especially true when using it for scholarship, personal study, or research. After all, the library exemption section of the Copyright Act explicitly authorizes copying entire works when they cannot be obtained at a fair price.[25] (Since the purpose of copyright is to give incentives to creators, the "fair price" provision must require that the work be available from the creator or her distributor at a reasonable price, not merely from a used book dealer.)

A copyright owner's refusal to permit the use of her work in a class, even after the offer of a permission fee, raises a thorny problem involving a copyrighted work's availability. The issue is particularly troubling when a copyright owner refuses permission because she does not like the circumstances of the use. In one instance that went to trial, the editor of a collection of interviews with women who had considered abortions refused an abortion opponent's request to quote them. Those who think of copyright primarily as a property right tend to think that refusing access is a prerogative of ownership. But the constitutional purpose of copyright is to provide creators with an incentive to make work available to the public, in the words of the Constitution, "to promote the Progress of Science and useful Arts." It is not intended to inhibit the pursuit of knowledge by fostering censorship. Where the work has already been published, the law recognizes no "moral right" of creators to refuse permission to use it. The question is whether a use is fair based on the four factors specified in the Copyright Act. If the historian is confident that her use is fair in light of those criteria, she should not be intimidated by a demand to desist.

But one should exercise greater restraint in the case of unpublished work. The fact that a work is unpublished always militates against fair use. In a well-known case, the famously reclusive author J.D. Salinger was able to prevent an unauthorized biographer from quoting his letters. No one doubted that Salinger cared more about his privacy than the market value of his correspondence. But the court thought the unpublished nature of the work trumped the biographer's critical and historical purpose.[26]

The law applies the fair-use doctrine to both published and unpublished work, but as the Salinger case indicates, there is a strong judicial tradition of guaranteeing to creators the freedom to decide whether, when, and how to make their work available—a principle called "the right of first publication." However, this principle is by no means a total bar to a finding of fair use. If the other criteria weigh on the side of fair use, quotation from unpublished material will be ruled fair.

The right of first publication applies with particular force to material that its creator chose not to publish or told recipients to keep confidential. It should carry less weight where the question never arose, as in the private correspondence of those who never achieved the kind of prominence that would make their letters valuable and who did not ask that they be kept secret. In such cases, the scholarly or educational purpose of the use should outweigh the unpublished nature of the copyrighted work, especially if the historian quotes only a small portion of the whole.

(3) *The amount and substantiality of the portion used.* The amount and quality of material borrowed from the original is also a factor in deciding whether a use is fair. It is particularly problematic to claim a right to use a copyrighted work in its entirety. This raises a real problem for the historian wanting to use a cartoon, painting, chart, graph, short poem, or song in a scholarly or educational publication. Publishers often insist that authors secure permission to even briefly quote poems and songs, or to reproduce

paintings or cartoons that remain in copyright. It is probably well to do so if the price is not exorbitant. Using the entirety of the work will weigh heavily against fair use, and a reasonable permission cost can easily be incorporated into the price of the book.

The situation is different in the case of a teacher-distributed coursepack or class website. Using the whole work in the case of visual art, cartoons and illustrations, charts, and graphs, or even a part of a short poem or song lyric, does tend strongly against fair use. Nonetheless, factors relating to the other criteria may outweigh this one. The *purpose* is clearly to promote nonprofit education. As to the *nature of the work*, charts and graphs are factual in nature and thus the preferred subjects of fair use. Political cartoons, while artistic and creative, are primarily designed to clarify or illustrate factual situations and to make political statements. In the case of paintings, poems, and song lyrics, the originals are intended for another purpose entirely and their use in a history class does not duplicate their artistic function. Nor is the use likely to affect the *marketability of the original.*

When one utilizes only a part of a copyrighted work for educational or scholarly purposes, how much is too much? It may be very little, if it appropriates "the heart" of the work. In a key case that found against fair use, the offending photocopying shop had published between seventeen and ninety-five pages from individual works, ranging from 5 percent to 30 percent of the total work. Of course, additional factors also weighed against the use being fair.[27] An agreement negotiated between representatives of publishers and some educational institutions at the time Congress passed the Copyright Act of 1976 permitted a very minimal amount of copying for classroom use: 250 words of poetry; articles up to 2,500 words long, and up to 1,000 words or 10 percent of other prose works, whichever is less; and one chart, graph, diagram, cartoon, or picture per book or periodical issue.[28] This so-called Classroom Guidelines agreement has no force of law and drastically understates the amount of copying that might be considered fair. But it should provide a safe harbor for those who adhere to it.

Like other factors, this criterion can relate to market value. A teacher cannot photocopy or post so substantial a part of *The Autobiography of Malcolm X* that one would reasonably conclude that students should have been told to purchase the book itself. The effect on the marketability and economic value of the original, combined with the large amount of the original used, will outweigh the educational nature of the use.

An article in an anthology, a collection of essays, or a journal is considered a single unit. Some analyses and guidelines discuss the amount that can be copied or distributed in terms of the entire collection or journal number, suggesting that a teacher copy or distribute no more than one article. However, it will always weigh against fair use to copy or distribute an entire article to a class, to post it on a class website, or to put it on electronic reserve, even if access is limited to students. Photocopying an entire article for private study or research, with no further distribution, is a different matter, as the exemption granted to libraries to provide such a service makes clear.

When quoting a copyrighted source in his own scholarly work, the historian should provide pithy quotes rather than extended ones, unless quoting at length is necessary to his analysis. When historians place excerpts from sources on reserve, post them on a class website, or reprint them in a classroom reader, the point is to convey their essence to our students. This runs against the rule that appropriating "the heart" of the original work, even though quoting only a few words, militates against fair use. It is inappropriate to apply this rule to historical scholarship or education, however. The notion that it is unfair to appropriate the heart of a work was stated particularly forcefully in what has become a leading copyright case, *Harper & Row v. Nation Enterprises.*[29] In that case *The Nation* scooped *Time* magazine's publication of excerpts from former President Gerald Ford's forthcoming memoir, and Ford's publisher sued. *The Nation's* editors claimed that it was a fair use for the purpose of journalism to publish a detailed report on the memoir's most important revelations even before it appeared in print, including brief but highly illustrative quotations. The Supreme Court's decision stressed that although brief and few in number, the quotations lay at "the heart" of President Ford's memoir, rendering their use unfair. The circumstances in which historians excerpt "the heart" of a source are entirely different, and central to the purpose of education. Appropriately limited excerpts should not be ruled unfair on this basis.

(4) Finally, the historian must take account of *the effect of the use on the potential market and value of the original work*—in other words, the economic effect of the use. If a use significantly compromises the creator's ability to profit from marketing her work, it will weigh heavily against the other factors that might support a claim of fair use. The user must consider not only what the copyright owner might lose on this particular occasion. She must also ask herself whether others are likely to make the same use. If so, what would be the cost to copyright owners? It is not fair use for a teacher to post small

portions of different textbooks on his website in lieu of assigning one. If the practice spread to other teachers, there would soon be no incentive to develop new textbooks. In fact, an all-electronic reading list, with no permission fees paid to publishers or books assigned for purchase, would probably not be a fair use of copyrighted work. Not only would it affect the market value of copyrighted works in general, the purpose would be seen as economic—to reduce the costs of class reading materials—rather than educational.

The potential effect on the marketability of a work is particularly relevant when putting parts of it on e-reserve, posting it on a class website, or including it in a reader. That is why the distribution of photocopied material through a profit-making photoduplication service is almost never fair use. The economic effect of such widespread photoduplication upon the marketability of the originals would be devastating. By enabling such easy and widespread copying and distribution through the Internet, the digital revolution creates a similar danger, even when those posting material have no commercial purpose. Therefore the first rule in making excerpts available in a reader, through electronic reserve, or on a class website is to restrict distribution to students enrolled in the class. This step is essential to limit the economic impact of the use as well as to assure that the purpose remains educational. Moreover, once the course ends, students' access to the material must end too.

Even if the distribution is limited, excerpting too much from a copyrighted work can weigh against its being considered fair use under the economic-impact criterion as well as the amount-of-the-source-used criterion. If one excerpts a small proportion of a work that one would not require students to purchase in any case, the loss to the copyright owner is minimal, and certainly does not equal the cost of the book, which would not have been purchased anyway. It will not weigh heavily against an otherwise fair use. But if the excerpt amounts to a significant proportion of the original, then the instructor should consider assigning the book itself. If the concern is to keep students' costs down, then paying a small fee for permission is the best approach. Moreover, securing permission to reproduce portions of books is becoming ever easier through the establishment of clearance centers accessible online.

Until recently, the marketability factor did not bear heavily upon excerpts from articles published in humanities and social science journals. Individual articles in these fields had little market value. But as more and more journals have joined permission clearance centers, individual articles have developed a market value derived from permission fees themselves. The question is no longer whether students should have been expected to purchase the relevant issue of the journal in which an article appeared, which plainly would be impractical. The question is whether the instructor should have paid the small fee incident to automatically securing permission.

The concept of clearinghouses to provide automatic permissions for the use of copyrighted work first sprouted in the music industry. One should check with the relevant agencies to learn the fees for distributing song lyrics or audio or video performances to students. If the cost is truly prohibitive, a case may be made for fair use on the ground that the only alternative would be to forego the use, which would bring the copyright owners no income in any case. If the purpose is clearly educational, the use may be considered fair (with all other criteria taken into account). It would be a close call, however, and a teacher might well consider whether another item, available at a more reasonable fee, might prove an adequate substitute.

The spread of copyright permissions clearinghouses is increasingly becoming a factor in considering the economic effect of a use. One can no longer simply ask whether students should have been required to purchase the book from which a reading was drawn. Instead, one has to ask whether one should have secured automatic permission from a clearance center for a reasonable fee. It is easy to incorporate the cost of permissions in the price of a photocopied class reader, and a commercial photoduplication service will do so in any case.

It is now customary to incorporate the costs of permissions into the price of classroom readers rather than to quibble over fair use. Many copyright owners argue that the same custom ought to apply when materials are distributed in class, put on a class website, or placed on electronic library reserve, because all these uses likewise diminish the market value of the original works. But the situations are not identical. It is awkward and contrary to the teacher-student relationship for a teacher to demand payment from those enrolled in her class. Requiring a teacher to pay permissions fees out of her own pocket imposes a burden that is likely to outweigh any economic benefit that would accrue to individual copyright owners from permission fees. It is legitimate for teachers to take these facts into account when evaluating whether a use is fair under the economic-impact criterion.

Creators and their distributors might argue that educational institutions ought to establish special funds for the purpose of securing such permissions. But the fair-use exemption for nonprofit education is expressly intended to promote instruction by sparing teachers and students some of the costs imposed by the copyright regime. Until courts decide otherwise, a teacher does not violate her ethical obligation to obey copyright laws by treating such a use as fair. Whether she or her institution is comfortable risking legal liability and the chance of litigation in such circumstances is a different matter. And if courts eventually rule against such a justification for fair use under the economic-impact criterion, or if Congress changes the statute, schools may have to devise some way to fund permission payments or transfer the cost to students.

If the publisher of a source that an instructor hopes to distribute has not joined a permissions clearance center, the teacher can compare the potential loss the copyright owner will bear to the burden placed on the education process if one has to choose among purchasing the original work, spending inordinate time and effort trying to negotiate a permission fee, or foregoing its use entirely. Such an evaluation generally reinforces the sense that excerpting a textbook for class distribution is not a fair use. Not only is the function of the textbook similar to that of the excerpt, but the textbook derives its value from the same market. In contrast, a work that is aimed at an entirely different market—a poem, a work of fiction, a photograph, or a work of art—is not likely to suffer in marketability or market value when incorporated into classroom materials.

Downloading excerpts from copyrighted work for personal research does not raise the problem of impairing marketability so starkly. Nonetheless, the historian should avoid photocopying large portions of a copyrighted book even for personal study and research. If borrowing the library's copy does not meet his needs, he should buy a copy of his own. Extensive photocopying would be justified only if the work is not available commercially at a reasonable price. And "reasonable" does not mean "cheap." It means within the bounds of reason, even if expensive.

Marketability can be a factor in whether quoting copyrighted work in one's own publications is a fair use. Brief quotation will rarely harm the original's market value. Nor perhaps would the reproduction of a photograph or cartoon. Nonetheless, if one can secure permission to reproduce such material at a reasonable price, it is best to pay it. Publishers will generally insist on securing permission to reprint such items in any case. The fact that most unpublished letters from ordinary correspondents lack market value will generally weigh in favor of fair use if the historian quotes from them. But an unpublished Vietnam War diary, or a letter describing the gathering at Grant Park in Chicago on the night Barack Obama was elected president, may well have some value. It would be prudent not to quote too extensively from such sources without permission.

FAIR USE AND LIBRARY RESERVES

Under the first-sale doctrine, a library may lend students physical copies of the works it owns, those it has borrowed, and those provided by an instructor without implicating copyright law. Those materials may be placed on reserve for students simply to read. But the authority to establish paper or electronic reserves from which students make copies depends on meeting the standards of fair use. The statutory exemptions for libraries are not applicable. They provide immunity from liability only when making copies for patrons for *individual* study, research, and scholarship. They do not authorize photocopying or digitizing for the use of others. Moreover, the copying cannot be systematic, as may be the case when students copy or download from library reserves. Until Congress creates a provision to accommodate library reserves, the usual four factors that govern fair use must be applied to any photocopying or digitizing the library or instructor undertakes to prepare such reserves, as well as to the photocopying or downloading students engage in to take advantage of them.

The reserve system must serve a nonprofit, educational purpose. Of course, any reserve system that serves a particular class will meet that criterion. The works placed on reserve for copying or downloading must be of an appropriate nature. Instructors should avoid including textbooks, course readers, and similar materials. The proportion excerpted from the copyrighted original should not be excessive. The effect on the market value of the original must be considered. It is particularly important to consider this last factor because of the systematic nature of copying from physical reserve shelves or downloading from digital reserves. Systematically copying and downloading work for which permission could be secured easily and at a reasonable cost is problematic.

The Copyright Clearance Center, which represents the interests of copyright owners, insists that electronic reserves are identical to course packs. The center stresses the obligation to secure permission for the copyrighted material placed on such reserves, implying that fair-use principles have only a narrow application to them.[30] A number of library associations, on the other hand, have circulated guidelines urging broad application of fair-use criteria to electronic reserves.[31] Worried about potential liability, many university and college libraries now require that requests to put material on reserve go through copyright specialists, who check whether the library has a license to reproduce holdings electronically—as is usual, for instance, with journal databases. In the absence of a license, they consider whether a request meets the criteria for fair use. If it does not, they inform the teacher. They may explore what it would cost to secure permission, and they may even have a fund to pay for it.

SECURING PERMISSION
TO USE COPYRIGHTED WORK

The information revolution has made copyright ownership more lucrative than ever before. The result is increasing sophistication in the marketing of permissions. No longer does a teacher or scholar have to contact each publisher of the material she wants to quote at length or use in class. Instead, publishers and other media companies, which generally acquire broad rights from creators, have joined clearinghouses that facilitate the acquisition of permissions and payment of fees, emulating the long-standing clearinghouses for musical compositions and performances. Huge archives of photographs and graphics can now be found online and licensed for use. This has made it possible for campus photocopy shops to secure permissions quickly and easily, especially for textual materials, and using these shops probably remains the easiest way to distribute classroom materials.

Securing a license to use music is also relatively easy. The law explicitly allows the reproduction of music in class or for remote learning. But if a historian wants to include music in a class website, she will have to secure permission if she concludes that she is exceeding fair use (or does not want to take the risk of being challenged). Securing permission for artwork, photographs, and graphic materials like cartoons is more difficult, because the larger number of licensing agencies makes it harder to locate exact items. But the historian can scan these sites for similar material and, if she finds another item equally useful, license it instead.

The development of clearinghouses and licensing agencies has both positive and negative implications for historians. On the positive side, it is much easier to secure permission than it used to be. By putting thumbnail images online, photo archives also provide a useful source for finding images. On the negative side, clearinghouses and photo archives have been established primarily to serve profit-making enterprises that intend to distribute a creation widely. They seem to be less accommodating to a limited use of a copyrighted work for a nonprofit purpose. One may try to ask permission of the copyright owner directly, but he may have licensed away the right to agree to the request.

Eventually, educational institutions and nonprofit scholarly presses and journals may negotiate agreements with clearinghouses and photo archives, allowing teachers and scholars to more easily acquire permissions. Such agreements might replace our present reliance on fair use and the uncertainly associated with it. As of 2012 the Copyright Clearance Center is offering an Annual Copyright License that "provides the comprehensive coverage colleges and universities need to share information . . . , while respecting the intellectual property of others."[32] The center's ReadyImages service provides ReadyImages for Academia, a subscription service giving access to millions of professional images. It is hard to predict how cash-strapped universities will respond to these offers. For now, historians will have to weigh the uncertainty in a claim of fair use against the cost of simplifying matters by securing permission. Few claims of fair use will actually be challenged or even noticed by copyright owners, which does not justify unethical conduct but should encourage the historian to act on a reasonable conclusion that his use is fair according to the legal criteria.

There are a number of ways to secure permission to use part of a copyrighted work. Photocopy shops that specialize in serving teachers are experienced in securing permissions, and historians preparing classroom readers should utilize their services. They will incorporate the fees into the price of the reader. You may ask to be informed if a copyright owner is demanding an excessive amount for the use of any particular reading and, if a personal call to the publisher's permissions office or a more senior manager does not help, substitute another reading in its place.

Book publishers' contracts often hold authors responsible for securing permission for quotations and reproductions of copyrighted work. Historians should accept that responsibility for quotations from textual material. A knowledgeable historian may be more likely than a publisher to recognize that the quotation is a fair use. However, publishers should take responsibility for securing permission to use photographs, cartoons, and the like, unless they are in the public domain. Reproducing them is unlikely to constitute fair use, and securing licenses for such material, while easier than it used to be, is still more difficult for the novice than for experienced professionals. Some publishers will undertake this job anyway, despite the language of their contacts. Most journal editors have more experience securing permissions than their authors do, but the process must often be a cooperative endeavor, especially in the case of sources acquired from libraries and manuscript repositories.

The Copyright Clearance Center (**www.copyright.com**) is the best source for securing permission to use material published in books, newspapers, and magazines. Most publishers are members. If a publisher is not a member, the historian can place a "special order" and the center will seek permission on her behalf. Securing permission to use the lyrics of songs still in copyright or music from a CD in a class website is also relatively straightforward. There are licensing agencies akin to the Copyright Clearance Center dedicated to music. The American Society of Composers, Authors and Publishers (**www. ascap.com**) and Broadcast Music, Inc. (**www.bmi.com**) license lyrics and songs themselves. That enables scholars to quote them and musicians to perform them. The Copyright Act authorizes teachers to play CDs and videos of performances in classrooms or long-distance teaching without paying for permission, but this concession does not cover websites. If a teacher wants to go beyond the limits of fair use in embedding an audiovisual in a website, the Harry Fox Agency (**www.harryfox.com**) licenses musical work for digital reproduction. The right to reproduce films and video on a website has to be secured from the creator or commercial distributor directly.

Securing permission to use a cartoon, an image of an artistic work, or a photograph is not as easy as securing permission to use literary or musical works. There are a number of databases that specialize in images, and if one is seeking permission for a particular image, it can take some work to discover which agency has been authorized to license its use. But one may find similar images that will do just as well. Corbis Images (**www.corbisimages. com**) has the largest database of photographs, including the great Bettman Archive. Bridgeman Art Library (**www.bridgemanart.com**) includes many photographs in its database and is probably the best source for images of fine art. Getty Images (**www.gettyimages.com**), owned by the *Washington Post*, is another good source for photographs. Editorial cartoons that remain under copyright protection usually provide the name of the cartoonist's agency somewhere on the panel. The quickest way to secure permission to reproduce them is to contact the agency, which may itself provide consent or explain how to contact the cartoonist. There are other creative ways to proceed. Investigating permission to reproduce a cartoon by the great "Herblock" (Herbert Block) via Google led me to *Herblock's History*, published online by the Library of Congress. Clicking on images from the exhibit led to an "object checklist," which gave the address for securing permission to reproduce the image. The time and effort invested in such an endeavor is a good reason for historians to take advantage of the principle of fair use.

PLAGIARISM AND COPYRIGHT

In the words of the AHA's *Statement on Standards of Professional Conduct*, plagiarism is "the expropriation of another author's work, and the presentation of it as one's own."[33] Plagiarism may constitute an infringement of the original creator's copyright, but only if it appropriates the original expression. Less obvious, but no less an infringement, is direct and close paraphrase. Appropriating the organization through which the original author expressed her ideas—if combined with a suspicious similarity in language—may be an infringement. In all such cases, the injured creator may have recourse through copyright law.

However, if the plagiarist restricts herself to appropriating the original creator's insights, ideas, discoveries, and new information—without appropriating the way he expressed them—she has not violated copyright laws and they will not provide a remedy. Copyright protects the way ideas and information are presented, not the ideas and information themselves, no matter how much work went into developing them. Even in a clear case of plagiarism, the fair-use doctrine prevents liability when its criteria are met. If the wrongful appropriation is clear, a judge probably would bend over backwards to find an infringing use of the original expression. But there are limits to how far one could harness copyright law against plagiarism. And copyright would not apply if an infringer plagiarized work that had been dedicated to the public or was in the public domain.

HISTORIANS AND THE
PENALTIES FOR INFRINGEMENT

As intellectual property has become more valuable, creators and distributors have lobbied Congress successfully to increase the penalties for infringement. These can be quite severe, including even criminal penalties. However, provisions exist to ease the concerns of historians and other educators. The law offers a good deal of protection for historians who act knowledgably and in good faith.

Historians and their institutions can infringe copyrights in three ways. They can directly infringe by exercising one of the rights reserved to copyright owners. They can be liable for a "contributory infringement" if they knew about an infringement and helped to make it possible. The institutions that employ them can be responsible for "vicarious infringement," if they infringe a copyright in the course of their employment and the institution has an economic interest in the outcome. Unless the historian has secured permission or has taken care to stay within the limits of fair use, she may contribute to a student's infringement by posting copyrighted work on a class website for students to download. Moreover, if her college has general supervisory power over her activities, it will have infringed the copyrighted work "vicariously," giving rise to "vicarious liability." The same definitions apply to those who infringe our work.

Penalties for copyright infringement can be severe. The injured creator, her publishers, or her distributors will almost always seek an injunction to stop the infringement temporarily while the case is tried. They can also ask to have existing copies impounded. The injunction can be made permanent if they win, and all existing copies destroyed. The owners of the copyright in the infringed work can sue for the actual damages they have suffered— the lost sales, licenses, and permission fees. They can also sue to recover whatever profits have accrued to the infringer.

Most infringements by historians probably will not cause very much in the way of actual damages. Infringing copyright in the course of preparing a bestselling textbook or popular history might do so, but making work available to twenty-five or fifty students will not. It will be difficult to assess

---

damages for infringing the copyright in an individual published article. There is not much of a market for them. The same goes for an unpublished letter, diary, or reminiscence. The copyright owner would have to prove market value. But putting portions of a $50 textbook on a website open to 100 students might generate $5,000 in damages if a judge determines that you should have assigned the original.

But even infringing the copyright of work without much market value can be costly. Because Congress intends copyright law to protect owners' rights even in works with little market value, it has enabled injured parties to sue for statutory instead of actual damages. The law gives judges great leeway in assessing statutory damages. They may award up to $30,000 for each infringement, as well as requiring the infringer to pay court costs and attorney's fees. If the judge finds the infringement "willful," he can impose an additional fine of as much as $150,000. But if one can demonstrate that the infringement was "innocent"—for example, if an infringer had good reason to believe the work was in the public domain or reasonably believed she was making fair use of the material—the judge can reduce statutory damages to $250 per incident.

Because even the reduced statutory damages might inhibit education, the law provides a special accommodation for educators and librarians, acting within the scope of their employment, who have infringed a copyright but who had reasonable grounds for believing their use to be fair. In such cases, judges are *required* to remit the statutory damages to zero. Nothing could make clearer why historians should learn about copyright law. Congress does not want the uncertainty and complexity of applying the doctrine of fair use to inhibit instructors from doing the best job they can for their students. But it protects only reasonable decisions made upon thoughtful consideration of the factors that determine whether a use is fair.

Before filing a suit to stop an infringement and secure damages, the copyright owner must have registered her work with the U.S. Copyright Office. Of crucial importance, a copyright owner can seek statutory damages and attorney fees only if she registered the infringed work within three months of publication. This grace period does not apply to unpublished work. Unless they registered the unpublished work before it was infringed, its creators can sue only for actual damages.

Nearly all published work will have been registered. But, fortunately for historians, primary sources such as private correspondence, diaries, and reminiscences rarely will have been registered. The actual damages for infringing such works will hardly ever be substantial enough to warrant litigation by the owner.

REGISTRATION AND NOTICE

One does not have to register one's creative work in order to receive copyright protection, nor does one have to place a notice of copyright on it. Creative work is protected by copyright from the time it is fixed in some medium, registered or not. However, a work must be registered before one can sue for its infringement. There are good reasons not to wait until that happens. Registration is prima facie evidence of ownership, and it precludes a claim of innocent infringement. Most important, only if one registers a work within three months of publication or before an infringement occurs can one sue for statutory damages and attorney's fees. The historian who has not registered her work in this way will have to bear the considerable financial burden of seeking to enjoin further infringement, if she decides to proceed at all. For much of our work, actual damages will not be substantial enough to make up for this cost, leaving us unable to take any action at all.

Historians usually think of copyright only in terms of their published work, and rely on publishers or journal editors to take care of registration. However, we also have copyrights in our syllabi, websites, unpublished manuscripts, written or taped conference presentations, lectures, and material we have prepared for classes. If we negotiate for them successfully, we may retain copyrights in digitally preserved lectures we prepare for distance learning. Few of us have even considered registering these kinds of work with the Copyright Office. But in a digital age we might find such work circulating without our knowledge or permission. Anyone might download material from our websites and distribute it. A student could circulate a syllabus, study questions, reading lists, or anything else we might post; colleagues could pass on a draft we sent to them for comment or handed out prior to a faculty workshop. Acknowledgment of our authorship may be stripped. Worse, material for which we do not want to be responsible might be added to work that bears our name. Work might be excerpted or shortened without our input, or used for objectionable purposes.

Registration is relatively cheap and easy, and only registration within three months of publication or before infringement provides the possibility of statutory damages and recovery of attorney's fees that make legal action viable. It is up each of us to decide what might be worth registering of the work we have prepared for classes or scholarship. Private companies offering copyright registration services online can be found simply by googling *copyright registration*. Historians can learn enough to register themselves by consulting the Copyright Office's "Registering a Work" (**www.copyright. gov/help/faq/faq-register.html**).

One follows the same basic procedure to register websites that one follows to register other work. Again, you can find companies who will do the work for you online, or learn more by consulting the Copyright Office's circular *Copyright Registration for Online Works* (**www.copyright.gov/circs/ circ66.pdf**), which gives specific instructions about how to describe online material. The Copyright Office has not issued regulations covering the deposit of materials transmitted online. It provides a number of alternatives, all described in the circular.

Although it is not necessary to display a copyright notice on one's work in order to receive copyright protection, doing so enables a would-be user to contact you for permission and precludes her from claiming an infringement was "innocent" in an effort to mitigate damages. The copyright notice should include the word "copyright," the abbreviation "copr.," or the copyright symbol © (*c inside a circle*); the year the material was first published; and the name of the copyright owner. Leave out the date if you are circulating an unpublished work to a limited group, but bear in mind that posting a work on a site for everyone to see may constitute publication. Place the notice in a prominent position where it will be seen.

Conclusion

In this information age, historians must learn the basics of copyright as part of their education as teachers and scholars. We have an ethical obligation to comply with the law and to respect the rights of copyright owners. We must be prepared to fulfill those obligations without sacrificing our legal rights or those of our students.

APPENDIX

DURATION OF COPYRIGHT

As time goes on, the copyright in more and more works will be protected for seventy years after the creator's death. If made for hire, copyright will expire 95 years after publication or 120 years after creation, whichever comes first. The same term will apply if the creator or the date of her death is unknown.

But because the 1976 Copyright Act gave different terms to works that had been protected under prior statutes, many works are subject to different copyright termination dates depending on when they were first published or created rather than when their creator died. The copyright term had expired for all works published before 1923. Works that had been published without a copyright notice between 1923 and 1977 had entered the public domain immediately. Those published with a copyright notice had been protected for twenty-eight years, with an opportunity for renewal. If the copyright in works published before 1964 was not renewed, they would enter the public domain when their first term ended. Nearly 80 percent of the work published between 1923 and 1964 is now in the public domain because copyright owners did not renew their copyrights. A later law made renewal for works published after 1964 automatic. The law made works that have been renewed eligible for sixty-seven more years of protection from the time of renewal. The first of these works will come into the public domain in 2018, ninety-five years after publication. There were a few other rules, noted in the table on the next page.

Duration of Copyright

When published or created	When protection begins	When protection ends
Published before 1923	In public domain	
Unpublished, creator died before 1932	In public domain since 2003; subsequent publication does not restore copyright	
Published without copyright notice between 1923 and March 1, 1989	In public domain, except for work published after January 1, 1978, that was registered within five years of publication	
Published with copyright notice between 1923 and 1963	When published	28 years. If renewed, extended 67 more years. If not renewed, now in public domain
Published without copyright between 1978 and March 1, 1989, but registered within five years of publication	When created	70 years after death of creator or shorter of 95 years from publication or 120 years from creation if work for hire
Unpublished, creator died after 1932	January 1, 1978	70 years after death of creator
Unpublished, creator unknown, date of death unknown, or work made for hire	January 1, 1978	120 years from date of creation
Unpublished in 1978 but published before 2003	January 1, 1978	70 years after death of creator, but no earlier than 2047
Created after 1977	When fixed in a tangible medium	70 years after death of creator or of last creator if a collected work
Created after 1977 for hire or by unknown creator	When published or when fixed in a tangible medium	Shorter of 95 years from publication or 120 years from creation

In most cases, the copyright status of a work published before 1978 depends on when it was first published, performed, or reproduced. This is easily determined in the case of text and recordings. The copyright date supplied in the front matter of books and journals will provide a close approximation (the copyright date can predate the actual publication date by a few months). So will the copyright date on a cassette or CD. Most but not all newspaper cartoons published since 1923 will carry a copyright notice. The creators of photographs published in books or periodicals should be credited, either where the photo is reproduced or in a separate photo credit section. The credit will sometimes give the date the photo was taken. It will at least give the name of the photographer and/or the present copyright owner. If a photograph taken before 1978 was published for the first time in a book, the book's publication date will mark the publication of the photo.

Remember that a work may be republished with a new copyright date, either because the copyright was renewed, or because the work was revised, or because other material was added. This is especially true of books. The later copyright date will pertain only to the renewal or to the revisions and additions. One can check WorldCat or the electronic catalogue of a major research library to try to find the earliest publication date.

Determining dates of publication can be difficult. Copyright in work published and copyrighted between 1923 and 1963 ran for a term of twenty-eight years, subject to renewal for a second term. Although the owners of only about 20 percent of eligible work renewed their copyrights, congressional statutes have provided them another sixty-seven years of protection from the date of renewal. To distinguish the 20 percent of works that have been renewed from the 80 percent that have not, one can contact the creator or publisher. It may be easier first to consult information provided by the U.S. Copyright Office, which provides catalogues of works that have been registered with the office. Although works do not have to be registered to receive copyright protection, any *renewal* of a copyright term *did* require registration. The office's Catalogue of Copyright Entries (CCE), published in print to 1978 and on microfiche to 1982, listed registrations of copyrights. Research libraries should have copies. Since 1982 the Copyright Office has put registration entries online (**www.copyright.gov**). Click Registrations and Documents under Search Copyright Records.

Researching the information provided by the Copyright Office works better for books and periodicals than for other kinds of copyrighted work, even though the CCE and the online catalogue document the registration of photographs, maps, art, and architectural plans—anything that has been registered. To find such information, one has to know the name of the registrant or the title of the work. Who knows how the copyright owner might have registered a particular photograph of Reverend Martin Luther

King during the Montgomery bus boycott or the March on Washington? A search under the title "Martin Luther King" will result in a number of photographs listed without illustrations to help identify the correct one. It is easier to choose a photograph from one of the online commercial databases.

Was the copyright renewed in a 1945 article you wish to distribute in class? Very few articles are ever registered with the Copyright Office either originally or when renewed. Most were copyrighted as part of the number of the journal in which they appeared. One can search the Copyright Office records to learn whether the copyright in the relevant journal number was renewed. But even if it were, one cannot be certain that the author transferred the copyright to the journal. In this case, if the journal is still active, it is better to contact the present editors.

Nowadays, a historian often finds images of photographs, cartoons, and other items on the Internet, where publication information may not be provided. One must be creative. Look for other copies online that might provide the information. Check the holdings of commercial image banks. One or more of them may have the image on its database and may give information about when it was created and who owns the copyright. Image banks often are licensed to sell permissions to reproduce copyrighted images, so you can simply pay them for a license to do so. But you may find that an image is in the public domain and thus can be used freely after all, or you might try to acquire permission at less expense directly from the copyright owner (see the section on Securing Permission, pages 41–43).

Tracking down publication information for work created before 1978 may require the same approaches as those described in the Securing Permission section.

NOTES

1. In a fuller discussion of the rival approaches to copyright, Paul Goldstein refers to copyright "optimists," who want to maximize returns to creators, and copyright "pessimists," who would hold returns down to the minimum that would assure continued creative production. Goldstein, *Copyright's Highway: From Gutenberg to the Celestial Jukebox* (Palo Alto, CA: Stanford University Press, 2003), 10–28.

2. Copyright Act of 1790, 1 Stat. 124 (1790).

3. Copyright Act of 1976, Pub. L. 94–553, 90 Stat. 2541 (1976).

4. Digital Millennium Copyright Act of 1998, Pub. L. 105–304, 112 Stat. 2860 (1998).

5. Berne Convention Implementation Act of 1988, Pub. L. 100–568, 102 Stat. 2854 (1988).

6. While federal copyright law was always limited to congressional statutes and their interpretation, before 1978 state law governed certain aspects of the subject. Analysts often called this state jurisdiction "common-law copyright." The 1976 act explicitly preempted copyright from state jurisdiction, although creative lawyers have since argued with some success that if the Copyright Act does not secure protection to a category of work, then state authority has not been preempted. Thus state law still governs some types of work created before the federal government extended copyright protection to them. Also other areas of law under state jurisdiction touch on matters closely related to copyright. Nonetheless, copyright in the United States is governed almost entirely by federal statute as interpreted by the courts.

7. The copyright statutes are title 17 of the United States Code, cited as 17 U.S.C.

8. 17 U.S.C., § 106 (2007).

9. 17 U.S.C., § 1101 (2007).

10. Hoehling v. Universal City Studios, Inc., 618 F.2d 972, 974 (2d Cir. 1980).

---

11. See Stephanie L. Seeley, "Are Classroom Lectures Protected by Copyright Laws? The Case for Professional Intellectual Property Rights," *Syracuse Law Review* 51, (no. 1, 2001): 163–89, for a fuller discussion of the issues.

12. The provisions were a controversial part of the Digital Millennium Copyright Act, now embodied in 17 U.S.C. 12 (2007).

13. Feist Publications, Inc. v. Rural Telephone Service Co. Inc. 499 U.S. 340 (1991).

14. Weinstein v. University of Illinois, 811 F 2d. 1091, 1094 (7th Cir. 1987); Hays and McDonald v. Sony Corporation of America, 847 F. 2d 412, 415 (7th Cir. 1988).

15. For more on the issue see Elizabeth Townsend, "Legal and Policy Responses to the Disappearing 'Teacher Exception,' or Copyright Ownership in the 21st Century University," *Minnesota Intellectual Property Review* 4 (2003): 209–83.

16. The complicated specifications of terms of copyright for unpublished works and works published at different times are established in 17 U.S.C. § 301–05 (2007).

17. Eldred v. Ashcroft, 537 U.S. 186 (2003).

18. The situations in which lapsed copyright may be restored are specified in 17 U.S.C. § 104A(h).

19. U.S. Copyright Office, "Exemption to Prohibition on Circumvention of Copyright Protection Systems for Access Control Technologies," last modified March 20, 2012, accessed May 7, 2012, **www.copyright.gov/1201** (accessed April 12, 2012).

20. 17 U.S.C., section 108 (2007).

21. The statutory language governing fair use, as amended, is at 17 U.S.C. § 107 (2007).

22. 17 U.S.C. § 504(c)(2).

23. 17 U.S.C. § 108(d)(1) (2007).

24. In one of the few cases involving the inclusion of excerpts from a copyrighted work in a course pack, the court evaluated "the propriety of the defendant's conduct" in assessing the purpose of her use of the plaintiff's work, and counted her failure to credit the author heavily against her. Marcus v. Rowley, 695 F. 2d 1171, at 1176 (9th Cir. 1983). Violations of scholarly conventions are not themselves violations of copyright, but this case provides a good example of how failure to observe them can affect legal decisions.

25. 17 U.S.C. § 108(e)(1). Note that the library exemption does not extend to making copies of unavailable work for *educational* purposes.

26. Salinger v. Random House, Inc., 811 F.2d 90 (2d Cir. 1987).

27. Princeton University Press v. Michigan Document Services, Inc., 99 F. 3d 1331 (6th Cir. 1996).

28. "Classroom Guidelines," in Copyright Clearance Center (CCC), "The Campus Guide to Copyright Compliance,"**www.copyright.com/Services/ copyrightoncampus/content/index_class.html** (accessed May 7, 2012). As an institution serving copyright owners, the Copyright Clearance Center takes a narrow view of fair use..

29. Harper & Row v. Nation Enterprises, 471 U.S. 579 (1985). At issue was *The Nation*'s scoop of *Time* magazine's publication of excerpts from the soon-to-be published diaries of former president Gerald Ford. *Time* had paid Ford and his publisher a substantial sum for the right to be the first to publish parts of Ford's manuscript. The Court forcefully repudiated *The Nation*'s argument that it had made fair use of the material for purposes of news reporting and criticism.

30. "Frequently Asked Questions about E-Reserves from the Association of American Publishers (AAP)," in CCC, "Campus Guide," accessed May 7, 2012, **www.copyright.com/Services/copyrightoncampus/content/library_aap.html**.

31. "Applying Fair Use in the Development of Electronic Reserve Systems," in CCC, "Campus Guide," accessed May 7, 2012, **www.copyright.com/Services/ copyrightoncampus/content/library_ers.html**.

32. Copyright Clearance Center, "Annual Copyright License for Academic Institutions," accessed May 7, 2012, **www.copyright.com/content/cc3/en/toolbar/ productsAndSolutions/annualLicenseAcademic.html**.

33. "Plagiarism," in American Historical Association, "Statement on Standards of Professional Conduct," last modified June 8, 2011, accessed May 7, 2012, **www. historians.org/pubs/free/professionalstandards.cfm#Plagiarism**.

Further Reading and Information

NOTE: Below are some of the more useful guides to copyright issues. Both the law of copyright and the environment of information technology are changing rapidly. Be sure to check for updated editions.

Websites

Columbia University Libraries/Information Services Copyright Advisory Office. **http://copyright.columbia.edu/copyright.**

Cornell University Copyright Information Center. **http://www.copyright. cornell.edu.**

U.S. Copyright Office. "Copyright." **http://www.copyright.gov.**

Handbooks and Guides

General

ABA Section of Intellectual Property Law. *What is a Copyright?* 3d ed. Chicago: American Bar Association, 2011.

Armatas, Steven A. "Basics of Copyright Law." In *Distance Learning and Copyright: A Guide to Legal Issues*, 25–110. Chicago: American Bar Association, 2008.

Fishman, Stephen. *The Copyright Handbook: What Every Writer Needs to Know.* 11th ed. Berkeley, CA: Nolo, 2011.

Gorman, Robert A., and Kenneth W. Gemmill. "Copyright Law: Second Edition." In *Copyright Law and a Brief Look at the Google Library Project*, edited by Brett D. Rhodes, 1–129. New York: Nova Science Publishers, 2010.

LaFrance, Mary. *Copyright Law in a Nutshell.* Saint Paul, MN: Thomson/West, 2011.

CLASS READERS AND ELECTRONIC RESERVES

Austin, Brice. *Reserves, Electronic Reserves, and Copyright: The Past and the Future.* Binghamton, NY: Haworth Press, 2004.

COPYRIGHT REGISTRATION

Warda, Mark. *How to Register Your Own Copyright.* 5th ed. Naperville, IL: Sphinx, 2004.

DISTANCE EDUCATION

Armatas, Steven A. *Distance Learning and Copyright: A Guide to Legal Issues.* Chicago: American Bar Association, 2008.

Lipinski, Tomas A. *Copyright Law and the Distance Education Classroom.* Latham, MD: Scarecrow Press, 2005.

DURATION OF COPYRIGHT AND SECURING PERMISSIONS

Armatas, Steven A. "Locating and Negotiating with Creators." In *Distance Learning and Copyright: A Guide to Legal Issues*, 235–311. Chicago: American Bar Association, 2008.

Bielstein, Susan M. *Permissions: A Survival Guide.* Chicago: University of Chicago Press, 2006.

Columbia University Libraries/Information Services Copyright Advisory Office. "Duration and the Public Domain." **http://copyright.columbia. edu/copyright/special-topics/duration-and-the-public-domain**.

Crews, Kenneth D. "Is this Book Still under Copyright?" **http://copyright. columbia.edu/copyright/2010/08/10/is-this-book-still-under-copyright**.

―――. "Researching the Copyright Status of a Book: Protected or Public Domain?" **http://copyright.columbia.edu/copyright/files/2010/08/ researching-the-copyright-status-of-books.pdf**.

Stim, Richard. *Getting Permission: How to License & Clear Copyrighted Materials Online & Off.* 3d ed. Berkeley, CA: Nolo, 2007.

FAIR USE

Armatas, Steven A. "The Doctrine of Fair Use and Education" and "Fair Use Guidelines for Educators." In *Distance Learning and Copyright: A Guide to Legal Issues*, 125–87. Chicago: American Bar Association, 2008.

Benedict, Michael Les. "Copyright I: Fair Use of Unpublished Sources." *Perspectives* 28 (April 1990): 1, 9–13.

Torrans, Lee Ann. "Unpublished Materials and Library Use." In *Law and Libraries: The Public Library*, 121–31. Westport, CT: Libraries Unlimited, 2004.

Wilson, Lee. *Fair Use, Free Use and Use by Permission: How to Handle Copyrights in All Media.* New York: Allworth Press, 2005.

FOR EDUCATORS AND WRITERS

Bielefield, Arlene, and Lawrence Cheeseman. *Technology and Copyright Law: A Guidebook for the Library, Research, and Teaching Professions.* 2d ed. New York: Neal-Schuman Publishers, 2007. Despite its title, this book is in fact a general guide to copyright for educators and librarians.

Butler, Rebecca P. *Copyright for Teachers and Librarians in the 21st Century.* New York: Neal-Schuman Publishers, 2011.

Crews, Kenneth D. *Copyright Law for Librarians and Educators: Creative Strategies and Practical Solutions.* 2d ed. Chicago: American Library Association, 2006.

Lee, Robert E. *A Copyright Guide for Authors.* Stamford, CT: Kent Press, 1995.

Lindsey, Marc. *Copyright Law on Campus.* Pullman: Washington State University Press, 2003.

Simpson, Carol. *Copyright for Schools: A Practical Guide.* 5th ed. Santa Barbara, CA: Linworth, 2010.

Wilson, Lee. *The Copyright Guide: A Friendly Handbook to Protecting and Profiting from Copyright.* 3d ed. New York: Allworth Press, 2003.

HISTORY OF COPYRIGHT

Goldstein, Paul. *Copyright's Highway: From Gutenberg to the Celestial Jukebox.* Stanford, CA: Stanford University Press, 2003.

Patterson, Ray L. *Copyright in Historical Perspective.* Nashville: University of Tennessee Press, 1968.

Rose, Mark. *Authors and Owners: The Invention of Copyright.* Cambridge, MA: Harvard University Press, 1993.

THE INTERNET AND COPYRIGHT

Hoffman, Gretchen McCord. *Copyright in Cyberspace 2: Questions and Answers for Librarians.* New York: Neal-Schuman Publishers, 2005.

Plagiarism and Copyright

Dames, K. Matthew. "Plagiarism is Different from Copyright Infringement." In *Copyright Infringement*, edited by Roman Espejo, 32–39. Farmington Mills, MI: Greenhaven Press, 2009.

Herrington, Tyanna K. "Authorship, Plagiarism, and Copyright." In *Intellectual Property on Campus: Students' Rights and Responsibilities*, 73–103. Carbondale: Southern Illinois University Press, 2010.

Posner, Richard A. *The Little Book of Plagiarism* New York: Pantheon, 2007.

Sterns, Laurie. "Copy Wrongs: Plagiarism, Process, Property, and the Law." *California Law Review* 80 (March 1992): 513–53.

Public Domain

Fishman, Stephen. *The Public Domain: How to Find & Use Copyright-Free Writings, Music, Art & More.* 5th ed. Berkeley, CA: Nolo, 2010.

Potter, Kenyon David. *An Educator's Guide to Finding Resources in the Public Domain.* Bloomington, IN: Phil Delta Kappa Educational Foundation, 1999.

Works for Hire

Crews, Kenneth D. "Instructional Material and 'Works Made for Hire' at Universities: Policies and Management of Copyright Ownership." In *The Center for Intellectual Property Handbook*, edited by Kimberly M. Bonner, 15–38. New York: Neal-Schuman Publishers, 2006.

Galin, Jeffrey R. "Own Your Rights: Know When Your University Can Claim Ownership of Your Work." In *Composition and Copyright: Perspectives on Teaching, Text-Making, and Fair Use*, edited by Steve Westbrook, 190–216. Albany: State University of New York Press, 2009.